Martin Gostelow

CONTENTS

This Way Corsica	**3**
Flashback	**5**
On the Scene	**11**
Ajaccio	**11**
Old Town 12, Place Foch 13, Palais Fesch 14, Iles Sanguinaires 15, Porticcio 15, Gorges du Prunelli 15	
The West	**17**
Tiuccia 17, Sagone 17, Cargèse 18, Piana 18, Porto 19, Gorges de Spelunca 21, Col de Vergio 21, Le Niolo 22	
The Southwest	**23**
Propriano 23, Filitosa 23, Sartène 24	
Bonifacio	**27**
Harbour 27, Upper Town 28, Boat Trips 29, Beaches 29	
The East and Centre	**30**
Porto-Vecchio 30, Solenzara 31, Aléria 31, Corte 33, Vallée d'Asco 35, Castagniccia 35	
The Northeast	**37**
Bastia 37, Cap Corse 39, Saint-Florent 42, Le Nebbio 42	
The Northwest	**45**
L'Ile-Rousse 45, Algajola 45, Calvi 46, Calenzana 47, Galéria 47	
Cultural Notes	**48**
Shopping	**50**
Sports	**53**
Dining Out	**55**
The Hard Facts	**58**
Index	64

This Way Corsica

Tucked into that corner of the Mediterranean where France and Italy meet, Corsica is close to both but unlike either. Strategically located 160 km (100 miles) southeast of Nice, the island attracted a procession of invaders. It has been fought over, bought and sold—treatments that only seem to have confirmed the character of the Corsicans as a people apart. Though they have latterly spent more than two centuries as a possession of France, it has had surprisingly little impact on them or their homeland.

The scenery is as spectacular as any in Europe; it would be hard to say which is the more breathtaking, the coast or the mountains. Sandy bays alternate with rocky coves where the water is crystal clear, often of a Caribbean turquoise hue. Granite cliffs turn flame-red in the setting sun, headlands are crowned by ancient watchtowers built to warn of the approach of pirates. That threat was the reason much of the coast was uninhabited then, and remarkably it remains so. People in the past gathered for protection in a few fortified ports—Bastia, Porto-Vecchio, Bonifacio, Ajaccio and Calvi—which are still the only big towns next to the sea.

Rugged Landscape

The interior is a land of infinite variety. Against a backdrop of high granite ridges and sharp pinnacles grow forests of tall pines, chestnut trees and vast areas of *maquis* scrub broken by rocky outcrops. Gorges cut deep gashes through the mountains, and the roads are few and tortuous. Here and there you come across a terraced garden of vineyards, citrus and olive groves. Ancient stone villages, deliberately built to be inaccessible, cling to the steep hillsides or the summits of crags. Many of them appear half asleep or abandoned. The rural population has long been in decline through emigration and you can see where the *maquis* has encroached on neglected fields and farms.

From the northwest near Calvi, the Parc Naturel Régional extends round the Gulf of Porto and down the spine of the island almost as far as Porto-Vecchio in the southeast. Covering more than a third of the area of Corsica, it offers a degree of protection to some of its most unspoiled and rugged scenery as well as the native fauna, including wild boar, big-horn sheep and many species of bird.

Seasons

For much of the year the island is tranquil, but summer transforms the scene, especially in July and August. If you like to be part of an animated crowd, love the buzz when all facilities are in full swing, want the sea to be warm and the sun scorching, this is the time for you. But prices are then at their peak, with accommodation hard to find without a reservation, and the narrow streets and even narrower mountain roads become overloaded with traffic.

By October, though the sea is still comfortable for swimming and the sun can give you a tan, the beaches are almost deserted and the roads empty. Many hotels close and in the others the rates plummet. Places that insist on a week's minimum stay in summer or require their guests to take half-board become completely flexible. Statistics say the rainfall is close to its maximum for the year, but it usually adds up to no more than three or four wet days. Wild cyclamen carpets the verges of mountain roads, enjoyed by a few walkers and cyclists who come to take advantage of the cooler weather.

Winter sees a sprinkling of snow on the summits, sometimes enough for skiing, though it's too unpredictable to create a regular business. Spring can be delightful, with a rush of wild flowers and the rivers full and fast enough to excite whitewater rafters.

Exclusively Corsican

The impact of tourism on the environment has been surprisingly limited. There is scarcely a single high-rise building, and few of the villa developments familiar elsewhere on Mediterranean coasts. Most hotels are locally owned and run, with no international names and only a couple of examples of the familiar French chain hotels.

Since the 1960s when the islanders began to notice that incomers were buying up land and property, many have refused to sell to outside interests, and some who might have thought of it have been put off by the fear of being ostracized. Through passive hostility or worse, potential purchasers have been deterred from even trying to acquire property, whether to settle permanently or to use as a holiday home. The Corsican language, related to the medieval dialects of northern Italy, is still widely used and adds to the air of exclusivity. None of this need worry you as a visitor. You're assured of a warm welcome, not only as the major means of support for the island economy but also because hospitality to strangers is an ancient tradition—as long as they come with pacific intentions.

Flashback

Early Days
Archaeological evidence shows that Corsica was inhabited as far back as 7000 BC. These first people probably came from northern Italy, sheltering in caves and living by hunting, fishing and gathering fruit and seeds.

Corsica's Stone Age monuments seem to have been the work of later arrivals from other parts of the Mediterranean, beginning in about 4000 BC. They built dolmens—groups of huge stones with one or more capstones on top—and erected menhirs, tall standing stones. The most elaborate of these are in human form, as at Filitosa, where some of the figures are shown carrying swords. These are the subject of debate: do they depict the people who sculpted them, or their leaders? Or, as some authorities suggest, their enemies? They may represent invaders who appeared on the scene around 1500 BC and have been given the name of Torréens, after the stone towers *(torri)* they built.

Greeks, Etruscans, Carthaginians and Romans
In the 6th century BC, settlers fleeing conflicts in Greece settled on the east coast near today's town of Aléria, but they promptly came under the influence of the Etruscans (from north of Rome). The great trading empire of the Carthaginians took over in the 3rd century, but its days were numbered. The rising power of Rome inevitably clashed with Carthage. The Romans soon seized the east coast of Corsica, although many more years were to pass before the interior was pacified. As well as a strategic possession and useful source of food, the island became a place of privileged exile for those whom the emperor wanted out of the way—but not so badly as to have them poisoned. Claudius banished Seneca to Corsica in 41 AD when his wife Messalina accused the philosher of adultery with Julia Livia, the emperor's niece.

Christianity arrived in the 2nd century AD and, after a period of persecution which created a number of local martyrs and saints, became the official religion of the empire early in the 4th century.

After the Fall
Six centuries of Pax Romana ended when the empire lost the ability to defend even colonies as close to home as Corsica, and it fell to Vandals from North Africa

FLASHBACK

Draped in a toga, Napoleon tames the lions in Ajaccio's Place Foch.

in 460. A Byzantine expedition recovered it, but not for long. The next four centuries were marked by the successive invasions of tribal groups that squabbled over possession of western Europe following the fall of Rome: Ostrogoths, Lombards and Franks. In addition, Moors from North Africa launched frequent raids and occupied a large part of the island for many years.

The Frankish leader Charlemagne had transferred sovereignty over Corsica to the pope in the 8th century, and in 1077 the reigning pope placed it under the Bishop of Pisa. (The Romanesque churches built by the Pisans are one of the glories of Corsican architecture to this day.) But local leaders in the mountains, usually out of step with the authorities in the coastal towns, were of two minds: some supported the papal decision, while others looked for backers in rival Italian cities, notably Genoa. In 1284, the Pisan fleet was defeated by the Genoese, who took control of the island, with scant regard for Corsican feelings. In another highhanded gesture, Pope Boniface then awarded the island to the Spanish kingdom of Aragon, and although they were unable to make good their claim—the Genoese simply ignored the Pope's decision—the Aragonese constantly looked for allies among the Corsican nobility and other leaders.

There were frequent rebellions against Genoese rule. In a bid to suppress them, in 1453 Genoa put the administration in the hands of a bank! But no ordinary bank; the Banco di San Giorgio had its own powerful army. Many of the towers still dotting the coastline were built at this time.

With French backing, a mercenary called Sampiero Corso managed to seize most of the island for short periods in the 1550s and 60s, until he was murdered, a victim of the vendetta. Such blood feuds were endemic throughout Corsican history—and are not unknown even today.

Brief Independence

Genoese rule—now direct rather than through the Banco di San Giorgio—was frequently challenged by local rebellions against taxes, land seizures and general arrogance. But the Genoese managed to retain control until 1729, when a major uprising spread right across the island and was contained only with the help of forces sent by the Holy Roman Emperor, Charles VI. When they left, fighting resumed

In 1736, Theodor von Neuhoff, a German opportunist, persuaded enough backers to furnish him with arms and gold and landed at Aléria, offering to support the anti-Genoese rebels. Obviously a born salesman, he managed to get them to declare him King of Corsica. But when his money ran out, and with no great military victories to show for it, he was forced to sail away after a mere eight months.

In 1738 the Genoese took the momentous step of calling on Louis XV of France to aid them against the Corsicans. The risings were quelled but, again, only until the French troops departed. Many of the rebel leaders had taken refuge in Naples. Among them was Pascal (or Pasquale) Paoli, who returned to Corsica in 1755 and succeeded in capturing all of the island apart from the coastal fortresses. Paoli introduced a new constitution, with an elected assembly and laws inspired by the liberal ideas which were sweeping Europe at that time.

But then the French returned to the scene, taking over the coastal towns still in the hands of the Genoese. Finally, in 1768, Genoa sold its claim to sovereignty over the island to France. A large French army landed, and within a year Corsican resistance was again crushed, Paoli taking refuge in London. On August 15, 1769, the future Emperor Napoleon was born in Ajaccio, the son of one of

Paoli's former aides, Carlo Buonaparte, and his wife Letizia of the important Ramolino family.

France Rules

In the 20 years that remained of French monarchy, France tried to be on good terms with Corsican leaders. As part of an assimilation programme, young Napoleon and his brother Joseph attended a military academy in France. When news of the 1789 Revolution in Paris reached the island, most Corsicans supported it and backed proposals for union with France.

British ships bombarded Corsican ports during the Revolutionary Wars—Nelson lost an eye while attacking Calvi. British troops occupied the north of the island in 1794, joining forces with none other than Pascal Paoli to declare an Anglo-Corsican kingdom. However, his supporters, known as Paolistas, wanted their own assembly, something rejected by the British viceroy, Sir Gilbert Elliott. The alliance fell apart, and in 1796 the British departed, leaving Corsica to the French who brutally suppressed any resistance. In 1814, Britain was briefly back again, but after the fall of Napoleon, the island was confirmed as French territory by the Congress of Vienna.

For the rest of the 19th century, despite road building, the opening of mines and two stretches of railway, economic development was at a low level. Agriculture remained primitive, malaria was endemic on the east coast and life was hard. Opportunities for the ambitious were mainly to be found in mainland France and in the growing French empire, a vast stage on which Corsicans could display their talents. The result was mass emigration and the plummeting of the island's population.

The 20th Century

French plans for improving the lot of the islanders were put on hold by World War I, and the war itself made matters worse by the carnage among Corsican conscripts. Mussolini's Fascist regime in Italy cast envious eyes on the island, such a close neighbour, and in World War II seized it with the aid of German troops. Following ancient tradition, local guerrillas took to the hills and the impenetrable bush, the *maquis*, whose name became attached to the resistance movement as a whole, including that in mainland France. With the Italian surrender in 1943, the Germans attempted to take over the whole defence of the occupied island, but it fell to the Allies later in the year.

After the war, the French government resolved to increase prosperity and turned to tourism as the principal opportunity for growth and employment. At first, most visitors were French, but word of the island's attractions soon spread and there was a modest boom. Ingrained local suspicion of outsiders led to some resentment and a general refusal to sell to "foreign" interests (and that included mainland French).

The Algerian War, resulting in the departure of a million French settlers from that huge territory, had a disproportionate impact in Corsica. Many thousands of *pieds-noirs*, as the displaced colonists were called, decided to put down new roots in the island. And the French Foreign Legion, whose base had been in Algeria, moved there as well. In retrospect, this was unduly provocative, with France appearing to treat Corsica like the colony it had just been forced to quit.

Fearing loss of control of their own destiny, many native Corsicans called for some degree of autonomy, ranging from an elected assembly to outright independence. A variety of political parties sprang up, from moderate to radical, and in 1976 the FLNC was formed, prepared to take direct action, including terrorism, to promote its aim of "liberation". The first shots were fired, triggered by nothing more than a wine scandal.

Some of the heat was taken out of the dispute in 1982 when Corsica became the first French region to have its own elected assembly, though its limited powers were not enough to satisfy campaigners for independence. In 1984, a renewal of the bombing of government targets and property owned by "outsiders" brought a crackdown by the authorities. The FLNC imitated other terrorist movements in using the proceeds of crime to finance its activities, and thereby lost some of its already minority support. A low level of violence continues, but following a split in the ranks of the FLNC, much of it is between rival factions, who indulge in old-fashioned vendettas. Meanwhile tourism flourishes in its delightfully understated fashion; climbing to more than 1½ million visitors a year— amounting to six times the permanent population.

1

THE GREATEST PREHISTORIC SITE Filitosa's standing stones, some of them sculpted with human faces and swords, are over 3,500 years old. Their dramatic setting is a secluded valley not far inland from Propriano.

On the Scene

Corsica is small enough to put every part within reach, but you will have to make choices: it would take a year to see it all. This guide covers the coastal towns and holiday areas, with ideas for excursions to the wild and mountainous interior. From the old capital, Ajaccio, we move up the west coast to the spectacular scenery near Porto. Then south, to Bonifacio; up the east coast to the port city of Bastia and Cap Corse; and finally the northwest coast around Calvi.

AJACCIO
Old Town, Place Foch, Palais Fesch, Iles Sanguinaires, Porticcio, Gorges du Prunelli

The most French of Corsica's towns sits in a sheltered, south-facing suntrap on the island's biggest bay. This was a long-time Genoese stronghold, when Corsicans were barred from living there. The French made it the headquarters from which they governed the island, and when Corsica was subdivided into two *départements* in 1975, Ajaccio became the administrative centre for Corse-du-Sud.

Ajaccio makes much of its role as Napoleon's birthplace, in spite of the reservations of Corsican nationalists, past and present, who have always resented his support for union with France. They all can take pride in another event, the liberation from Axis powers in World War II. When the Italian occupation forces effectively changed sides in 1943, the *maquis* resistance fighters seized Ajaccio and held it until Free French troops arrived in the famous submarine *Casabianca* to reinforce them.

A sightseeing tour is like a biography of the emperor and his family, but there is more to Ajaccio than Napoleonic monuments and museums. It has Corsica's biggest and best selection of restaurants, with hundreds of tables in the open air whenever the weather permits—and it usually does. Lining Place Foch, the waterfront and the streets of the old town, the eateries entice you with their appetizing menus and competitive prices.

Car ferries from Marseille, Toulon and Nice tie up at the quay right in the town centre, often with a sleek cruise ship in the next berth. Pleasure craft pack the two marinas, one below the citadel's walls, the other at the north end of the long waterfront.

Old Town

The main gate of the walled Genoese town once faced Place Foch. The gate and walls have long disappeared, but the narrow streets still follow the original pattern. Some bear the names of members of Napoleon's family, including the central Rue Roi de Rome, and their house stands right in the middle.

Citadel

The blunt peninsula where the old town stands is tipped by a typical 16th-century fortress with low, thick walls and sharply pointed bastions. It was begun during the brief French occupation from 1553–59 and completed by the Genoese when they returned. It has long been a French army base and is not open to the public. The troops use the flat bottom of the dry moat to play volleyball, while helicopters come and go about their business, clattering noisily. Below the wall on the seaward side is a small stretch of sand, the nearest beach to the city centre.

West of the citadel, the seafront Boulevard Lantivy is lined every Sunday by the stalls of a flea market. Steps lead down to a narrow beach, surprisingly clean and pleasant given its proximity to the city.

Maison Bonaparte

In the middle of the old town in the narrow Rue St-Charles is the large house where Napoleon was born on August 15, 1769. It has a chequered history: when the Bonapartes were forced to flee in 1793 after switching sides to support French rule rather than Paoli's nationalists, it was scraped clean of any vestige of the family. Napoleon's mother Letizia later returned and restored it, but did not stay. Her descendants gave it to the French nation in 1924.

Apart from her wooden sedan chair, near the entrance, there's little to see on the ground floor. Upstairs on the first floor, a rambling range of reception rooms is filled with mostly reproduction furniture, and the sofa on which the future emperor was brought into the world. The main exhibition is on the floor above but consists largely of replicas: portraits of his parents and countless relations, and other relics. The sword he wore as lieutenant-colonel and some fine pistols owned by his father Carlo are originals, but only uncritical Bonapartists will be interested in some of the more abstruse exhibits, accumulated after the best had already been snapped up by other museums and the many private collectors in this field.

A huge family tree traces the Napoleonic succession to the present day, and it's clear that there is no danger of the line dying out. The current claimant, accorded the title of His Imperial Highness Prince Napoleon, is a descendant of the first emperor's brother Jerôme.

Cathedral

Not far away, through the narrow streets of the old town with their numerous craft shops, stands the 16th-century cathedral, where Napoleon was christened in 1771, aged 23 months. The Renaissance interior is embellished by a marble altar, brought from Lucca in Italy in 1811 by his sister Elisa. There is a painting of the Virgin by Delacroix in the chapel to the left of the altar.

Place Foch

On the edge of the old town, Place Maréchal-Foch stretches up a gentle slope from the waterfront, by way of an attractive palm garden. Near the top, four granite lions support a marble Napoleon as First Consul, pompously dressed in a Roman toga. Above the tourist office at the lower end of the square is a small Napoleon Museum with a collection of memorabilia, including his certificate of baptism and a replica of his death mask.

Market

The island's biggest market is held every morning except Sunday in Square César-Campinchi, behind the town hall, next to Place Foch. Stalls are piled high with flowers, fruit and vegetables, fish, local cheeses, hams and other island delicacies such as honey, wines and liqueurs.

More Napoleons

West of Place Foch, the vast Place Général-de-Gaulle is locally called by its older name, Place du Diamant. Facing the square, Napoleon as a Roman emperor on horseback lords it over his four brothers in the togas of lesser dignitaries. The memorial's base is favoured by writers of graffiti, both political and scatological.

Yet another monument to Napoleon stands on Place Austerlitz at the top end of the avenue leading west from Place Foch. Booted and hatted, he broods above a list of his battles (only victories qualify) and his more lasting achievements—the legal code, the Bank of France and other state struc-

If you're looking for sun and solitude, head for the beaches of the southern Gulf of Ajaccio.

tures. An outcrop of granite next to the memorial shelters a "grotto" where he is supposed to have played as a child.

Palais Fesch

From the top end of Place Foch, Rue Cardinal-Fesch leads to the sprawling Palais Fesch, named, like the street, after Napoleon's uncle (his mother's half-brother), who for some years was archbishop of Lyon.

He accumulated great wealth, and used it to indulge his taste for art, buying thousands of Old Master paintings dating from the 14th to the 18th centuries. He left them to the city, but Napoleon's brother Joseph sold off some of the best, chiefly the Dutch, to raise money. Despite this, the remaining collection is one of the finest of its kind.

On Level 1, up the first flight of stairs, are mainly Italian and Spanish pictures from the 14th to 17th centuries. The stars for most viewers are Botticelli's *Virgin and Child*, a youthful work, and Titian's *Man with a Glove*. Level 2 has many magnificent still-life paintings and some huge canvases on religious themes. The pictures are strikingly displayed against stark white walls, but information about the artists or subjects is limited. The basement houses some minor Napoleonic memorabilia.

Facing the same courtyard as the museum is the Chapelle Impériale, the south wing of the palace built in the 1850s on the orders of Napoleon III. It became the last resting place of Napoleon's mother Letizia, his father Carlo and Cardinal Fesch, as well as several later members of the Bonaparte family.

Iles Sanguinaires

A scenic drive west from Ajaccio leads past a succession of beaches to the Punta de la Parata with its Genoese watchtower, one of many on the island. Late in the day, the offshore islets called Les Iles Sanguinaires glow blood-red in the setting sun. It's tempting to assume that they got their name that way, but it probably derives from their location, the south end of the Gulf of Sagone.

You can get there by boat from Ajaccio, landing at the biggest island and staying for an hour, time for a walk along the shore and up to the lighthouse on its peak, 80 m (263 ft) high.

Porticcio

A superb arc of sand facing the bay south of Ajaccio benefits from plenty of public parking space next to the beach. It's needed when crowds pour out from the city on summer days, joining the holidaymakers staying at the hotels and camp sites just a short walk away. Bars, beach cafés, clubs and discos add to the lively scene.

Southern Gulf of Ajaccio

South of Porticcio, the beaches are just as beautiful, and become progressively quieter the further you go. Plage d'Agosta has a handful of hotels and villa developments; Plage de Ruppione is a sheltered cove, usually with calm clear water perfect for snorkelling. At Plage de Verghia and the little fishing port of Chiavari the main road turns inland; the coast road soon peters out near a Genoese tower on the headland of Punta de la Castagna.

Gorges du Prunelli

For a varied inland excursion, follow the valley of the Prunelli river back into the mountains, east from Ajaccio. Not far from the airport, the gentle lowlands are planted with citrus orchards. Higher up, these give way to groves of olive trees and then to *maquis* where semi-wild boars roam and herds of sheep graze the clearings; the ewes' milk cheeses (*brocciu*) from this area are renowned.

The river gorge really begins beyond the village of Ocana, with granite walls closing in on either side, topped with jagged pinnacles of rock. A dam below the pretty village of Tolla has created a huge, deep artificial lake. The road climbs through ever more rugged and wild country to Bastelica and beyond it to Val d'Ese, where winter snows can be heavy enough to activate the ski centre.

For a different return journey, take the high, twisting and superbly scenic road south of the gorge to Cauro, the junction with the main route from Ajaccio to Sartène.

Bastelica

A grim-looking mountain village of granite houses 40 km (25 miles) from Ajaccio, Bastelica nevertheless sees plenty of visitors. Some come for the famous hams, sausages and other *charcuterie*, some for the mountain scenery. And Corsican nationalists want to see the birthplace (in the adjoining hamlet of Dominicacci) of their hero Sampiero Corso (1498–1567), shown in a dramatic pose in a bronze statue near the modern village church.

NATIONAL HERO

"The most Corsican of Corsicans", according to an inscription on his birthplace in the village of Bastelica, Sampiero Corso first made his name as a mercenary soldier with the Medici rulers of Florence. In the entourage of Catherine de Medici, he went to France and saved the life of her husband, the future Henri II, earning royal gratitude and a promotion to colonel. Returning with fame and fortune to Corsica, he married a young noblewoman, Vannina d'Ornano, against the opposition of her brothers, and also incurred the suspicions of the Genoese, who put him in prison for a while. When war broke out between Genoa and France in 1553, Sampiero joined the French invasion force. With the help of Turkish ships under the command of the notorious pirate Dragut, and a widespread Corsican uprising, the French soon seized most of the island. Only Calvi held out, despite intense bombardment from land and sea.

In 1559, a peace treaty returned Corsica to Genoa, to the fury of Sampiero, by now in exile in France. Suspecting his wife of complicity with the Genoese, he murdered her. In 1564, he landed again in Corsica to raise a revolt, and succeeded in taking over most of the interior. But the Genoese held the ports, and put a price on his head. After three years of bitter fighting, Sampiero was betrayed and killed in an ambush arranged by his wife's brothers who had sworn to avenge her. His head was displayed at the gate of Ajaccio.

THE WEST

Tiuccia, Sagone, Cargèse, Piana, Porto, Gorges de Spelunca, Col de Vergio, Le Niolo

North of Ajaccio, two great bays cut into the west coast of Corsica. The Gulf of Sagone has the bigger beaches, with lush orchards and rich farmland on the gentler slopes inland. The Gulf of Porto is more dramatic, with rocky shores and a few sandy coves. In many places the mountains rise straight out of the sea just one narrow, winding road climbs through stunning scenery to the highest and wildest parts of the island.

Tiuccia

Genoese towers guard the north and south ends of a half-moon bay whose sandy shore has attracted a ribbon of hotels and beach cafés. Inland on a hill stands the ruined Castello Capraia, once a stronghold of the lords of Cinarca. Even better and much less developed than Tuccia is the huge Liamone beach, a short distance to the north, where the River Liamone meanders through marshes and sand dunes to the sea.

La Cinarca

Turn inland from the Gulf of Sagone, by one of the roads to the north or south of Tiuccia, and you'll soon be climbing terraced hillsides planted with vines and olive trees, orange groves and chestnuts. Cattle graze the roadsides and patches of pasture, but the picturesque villages—Casaglione, Sari-d'Orcino, Calcatoggio and a dozen tiny hamlets reached by narrow, twisting lanes —seem to be fast asleep. And yet this little Eden, shielded by mountains and watered by fast-flowing streams, was once the stronghold of the Cinarchesi, ambitious lords who aspired to rule the whole of Corsica, and almost succeeded. Best-known to history and legend is Sinucello della Rocca, or Giudice ("The Judge"), who briefly united the island's quarrelsome chieftains in the 13th century in resistance to the Genoese invasion.

Sagone

Once a powerful city and bishopric, Sagone was destroyed in repeated Saracen raids. The cathedral was demolished in the 16th century and the bishop and his retinue moved to the comparative safety of Vico, inland beyond a mountain ridge. Only a fishing village survived on the site until recent years, when its extensive beach encouraged hotels to open.

Rocky islets and coves attract divers; there's a diving school for those who want to qualify. The ruins of the cathedral stand to the north of the present village; two prehistoric menhirs can be seen built into the walls.

Cargèse

On a rocky plateau overlooking the Gulf of Sagone, Cargèse is partly populated by descendants of Greek immigrants who fled a Turkish invasion of their homeland in the 17th century. They have preserved much of their original language and many of their customs, songs, dances and religious festivals—one of the town's two Catholic churches is Greek, with a brightly painted interior and modern icons. A plaque in the doorway gives the history of the Greek community, but only in French. The other church faces it across the valley; it has a naïve *trompe l'œil* ceiling. Of the many names on the 1914–18 war memorial inside, most are of Greek origin, although Italianized long ago. There is a fine view from the promontory and a long sandy beach below.

Piana

This pretty village perches on the hillside high above the south side of the Gulf of Porto, staying cooler in summer than the coast and yet within easy reach of some lovely bays and beaches. A couple of classic hotels were built in the 1930s and are functioning again after many years closure. What first made it a holiday centre was the extraordinary scenery, especially the unearthly rock formations of the Calanche.

A panorama of Piana, the gulf and mountains can be seen from the hilltop Belvédère de Saliccio, up a narrow track with a dozen hairpin bends.

The main beach, Plage d'Arone, is about 12 km (7 miles) to the west by way of a scenic route with views over the Gulf of Porto and the point that marks its southern limit, Capo Rosso, a dramatic pinnacle of red rock with its inevitable Genoese tower. A track signposted *Tour de Turghiu* leads down to it from the road; allow three to four hours for the testing round-trip hike.

Ficajola

To find the prettiest of all beaches in the area, look for the sign to Ficajola via route D624, a turn to the right off the road to Arone, which comes up soon after leaving Piana. A steep and tortuous road—hazardous even by Corsican standards—ends after 4 km (2½ miles) at a car park. From there it's a 4-minute walk to the beach, a tiny cove hemmed in by marvellously twisted and coloured rocks.

PIANA • PORTO

In a stunning setting of red granite, the little village of Piana.

Les Calanche

The craggy crimson granite cliffs and boulders of this spectacular region have been eroded by wind and water into fantastic spires, towers and arches. Some of these remarkable conformations are visible from the Piana-Porto road, an engineering achievement in itself; be forewarned that there can be quite a procession of traffic in summer. Fortunately, many parking spots have been provided. Still more amazing formations can be found if you are prepared to walk to reach them —heavy duty rubber-soled shoes are recommended. One sign by the roadside points the way to *Le Château fort,* but this is no castle made by human hands. About an hour's hike from the road, it's a massive pile of natural granite that looks like a fortress.

For another aspect of the Calanche, take a boat excursion from Porto; the trip takes about an hour. The formations look their most dramatic towards sunset, when they seem to glow as if red-hot, a reminder of the volcanic turmoil in which the rock was formed.

Porto

Painters and photographers love the colours and contrasts of rugged scenery and deep blue sea around the Gulf of Porto. In the arms of the bay nestles the holiday town of Porto itself, on the north side of a steep river valley, facing a Genoese watchtower on an outcrop of vivid pink rock. Across the river, reached by way of a hump-backed footbridge (or a road higher up), a marina for small craft has been carved out behind the wide beach of shingle and granite pebbles. Children collect them in almost all the colours of the rainbow: purple, crimson, orange, yellow and green.

Boat trips from Porto visit every part of the gulf, including stretches of coastline inaccessible in any other way. One excursion is to the cliff caves on its northern shore where the whole peninsula of Scandola is a nature reserve, a haven for eagles, ospreys and other rare species that nest on the rocky ledges and jagged pinnacles.

Girolata

The isolated fishing village of Girolata can only be reached by sea or an energetic walk, starting from Col de la Croix on the main coast road. It's possible to see the objective in the distance, on the second bay along the north shore of the Gulf, before following the signposted track down through the *maquis*. The walk to Girolata, estimated on the sign to be 1 hour 30 minutes, is about right for anyone keeping up a steady pace. The trail varies from smooth path to rocky scree, dropping at its midpoint to a weed-choked cove before climbing round the cliff to the bay of Girolata itself.

A handful of houses and a few boats are overlooked by one of the biggest surviving Genoese fortifications, on a rocky point made steeper by quarrying to improve its defensive qualities. The bay saw a significant naval action in 1538 when the Genoese admiral Andrea Doria trapped and captured the corsair Dragut, releasing many galley slaves although still more were drowned, chained to their oars when their ships sank. Dragut managed to pay the ransom to regain his freedom and resume his career: his release must have been regretted later when he became even more powerful, his ships a freelance navy which took part in the siege of Malta. It is believed that he personally ordered the destruction of Girolata. Certainly the 16th century saw much of this coast depopulated, and all but the strongest fortified ports were abandoned.

Partinello

The corniche road up the coast meanders high above the sea to the quiet village of Partinello, boasting a couple of attractive hotels and a few shops. The two nearest beaches, Caspiu and Gratelle, are a little further north, each about 5 km (3 miles) from the main road. With a mixture of pebbles, sand and shingle, they are sheltered and usually not too busy, even in high summer.

Gorges de Spelunca

The only road across the mountains of northern Corsica passes through breathtaking landscapes of deep gorges and jagged cliffs, pine forests and windswept uplands. It climbs steeply from Porto to Ota, a village hanging on the side of the Porto river gorge, then dives to cross the river by a modern bridge. The graceful arch of the old Genoese bridge can be seen just downstream; to reach it you'll have to make a short scramble down the bank.

From Ota to Evisa the road follows the Spelunca Gorge, a great gash in the mountains which rise on both sides to red pinnacles over 1,000 m (3,300 ft) high. Those who want to absorb its majesty at a gentle pace can walk the marked path that follows the gorge. Lower down than the road, it spends much of its length in dense woodland, so the view is often interrupted. The signs suggest a time of 3 hours, realistic if you don't make long stops. Naturally the downhill Evisa-to-Ota direction is less strenuous and more popular.

Forêt d'Aitone

Beyond the bright, cheerful mountain resort of Evisa, the D84 road enters one of the largest stands of Laricio pines in Corsica. Tall, needle-straight, slow-growing and therefore hard, these were long prized for use as ships' masts. The Genoese built the road to Porto so that they could get the massive trunks down to the sea. Beside the road 3 km (2 miles) from Evisa is a sign reading *Piscine*, pointing to a series of clear, natural pools formed in smooth slabs of rock by the Aitone waterfalls.

Free-range cattle graze the verges, herds of handsomely horned goats amble across the road without a care for the traffic. Family groups of semi-wild boars root about in the undergrowth, or in autumn munch the fallen chestnuts that carpet the ground.

Col de Vergio

As the road climbs higher, the forest gives way to dwarf conifers and then to almost barren granite. The top of the pass, Col de Vergio, is marked by a modern statue of Christ the Good Shepherd. A signposted footpath to the north leads still further, to the Bergeries de Radule, a 2½-hour round-trip. Keep an eye on the weather if you go walking; those clouds on the mountain summits all around can quickly close in.

The pass itself is 1,477 m (4,846 ft) high, and may be sprinkled with snow at any time between October and May, and occasionally blocked in mid-winter. But heavy falls seem to be getting rarer these days, so the oversized and ugly ski lodge just downhill sees little business.

Le Niolo

To the northeast of Col de Vergio the road descends through pine forest into the wide upper basin of the Golo, a river that eventually reaches the sea south of Bastia. Called the Niolo (from *niellu*, dark), the valley was for centuries the most isolated part of the island, never subdued by invaders in spite of vicious punitive expeditions.

Calacuccia

At the heart of the Niolo is a cluster of little villages. Calacuccia, the largest, comprises a scattering of sombre granite houses and an 18th-century church. The river was dammed in the 1960s and the land below the village is now a lake, supplying water to Bastia.

Traditionally, the people of the region were suspicious of strangers. Now, tourism being one of the few providers of new opportunities, they are making an effort to extend a welcome. Hotels, hostels, campsites and rooms in family homes (*chambres d'hôte*) offer a range of lodging, shops sell the local cheeses and *charcuterie*, and crafts are being revived.

Hikes and Climbs

Calacuccia's tourist office supplies maps and provides information on activities in the area, notably the walks—from leisurely strolls along the lakeshore to long-distance treks. Corsica's highest mountain, Monte Cinto, rises up 2,707 m (8,882 ft) to the northwest. Starting above the village of Lozzi, a strenuous hike to the top and back takes a full 12-hour day. It shouldn't be tackled without maps, provisions and the right clothing—the weather can change suddenly. Information on refuges is available at the tourist office, which can also recommend mountain guides.

Scala di Santa Regina

Apart from the high Vergio pass, the only route into the Niolo is a wild and narrow gorge to the east, where the Golo cuts through a ravine 300 m (1,000-ft) deep, the Queen of Heaven's Staircase. Until the 19th century it was traversed only by a tortuous 21-km (13-mile) track, with perilous sections where steps are cut into the cliffs. Then a road was built that is still a marvel of construction. Emerging from the gorge at its eastern end, it links up with the routes to Corte and Bastia.

THE SOUTHWEST
Propriano, Filitosa, Sartène

The southwest coast around Propriano has one of the biggest concentrations of holiday accommodation in Corsica. Not far inland are the dramatically sited mountain fastness of Sartène and the island's most significant prehistoric relics, the mysterious stone sculptures at Filitosa and Cauria.

Propriano

It may now be best known to visitors for its beaches and watersports, but Propriano is an ancient port with a history of action. Too much action, in fact, to have left many traces of its past. Used by the Carthaginians and Romans, it later served as the harbour for Sartène, the fortified town in the mountains 13 km (8 miles) inland. Propriano was repeatedly raided and burned by Barbary pirates and, like most small ports on these coasts, was eventually abandoned by its population who moved to safer spots in the hills.

Recent years have seen the growth of a rash of hotels and villas. Beaches east and west of the town are well provided with facilities, and there's a wide choice of restaurants.

There's a ferry connection to Marseille and Toulon from April to September, and a year-round service to Sardinia.

Filitosa

Corsica's major prehistoric site lies some 40 km (25 miles) by road south of Ajaccio between the coastal and inland routes to Propriano. The setting is superb, a secluded valley ringed by green hills, with a great granite outcrop standing guard in the centre. Its highest point is crowned by the remains of a tower dating from around 1300 BC, surrounded by traces of other buildings and ramparts. Tall columns of worn stone roughly shaped into human form, ranging in height from about 1 to 2 m (3–7 ft) gaze blankly over the landscape. More of the figures stand below in the meadows amid scattered boulders, olive trees and gnarled cork oaks.

Among the finest megalithic sculptures in existence, these have been dated to around 1700–1400 BC. Most menhirs (standing stones) from that era have little or no carved detail, but several Filitosa figures have clear facial features, and one or two are unmistakable phallic symbols. Even more unusual, some of them are shown bearing weapons—great swords held upright in front of them or daggers at their sides.

The figures lay unnoticed, hidden by vegetation, until 1946 when the local landowner stum-

It may look like a heap of stones to you, but Filitosa is an archaeologist's dream.

bled on one, and then several more. Serious excavation and restoration of the site started in 1954. Some of the menhirs had been re-used as mere building blocks in the tower and ramparts, so their positioning now is the result of guesswork by the archaeologists.

Museum
The small museum just inside the entrance is worth visiting before or after the site itself—ideally both. Three fine examples of the megalithic figures are on display; one from the nearby hillside village of Olmeto is shown wearing a helmet drilled with holes, perhaps meant to carry horns. Roger Grosjean, who headed the excavation, believed that the Neolithic carvers were depicting their enemies, the so-called Torréens who were eventually to conquer them. Not all archaeologists agree—the conventional view is that the statues honour their creators' own chieftains or perhaps their gods.

Sartène
Constantly threatened in the old days by the pirates of North Africa, the heavily fortified town of Sartène has preserved its medieval appearance around the massive granite Hôtel de Ville, once the palace of Genoese gov-

ernors. There are strange perspectives to be discovered from the narrow streets, staircases and archways opening suddenly onto a view of the sea below or, on the other side, the Rizzanèse valley.

Musée de la Préhistoire

Up a steep hill a short distance from Place de la Libération stands a grim granite blockhouse with tiny barred windows. If it looks like a prison, that's because it used to be one. Now it houses good, clear displays covering Corsican prehistory from 6,000 BC to roughly AD 200, arranged in chronological order in six main rooms. Among the most striking exhibits are gold jewellery from Neolithic tombs, flint and bronze weapons and two warrior statues of the type found at Filitosa.

Megalithic Sites

Suitably close to Sartène with its prehistory museum are some of Corsica's most impressive ancient monuments, although a shortage of signposts means that few people ever get to see them. If you are intrigued by the island's distant past, take the main road towards Bonifacio and just out of Sartène, at Bocca di Albitrina, turn right towards Tizzano. After 7 km (4 miles) a sign to the left points to Cauria. A narrow but paved road twists through the maquis for 4 km (over 2 miles) before a sign to the right *Dolmens et Menhirs* shows the way down a rough track (just passable for cars), 800 m (900 yd) to the first group of monoliths. Called the Stantari menhirs, they comprise 25 standing stones, more than 2 m (7 ft) high. Most have lost any carved details they may once have had, but two show traces of facial features and swords across their backs.

It's a 3-minute walk through the bushes to the Dolmen de Fontanaccia, the best-preserved monument of this type in Corsica. The box-shaped burial chamber enclosed by huge flat boulders is capped by a single flat stone, the whole structure being 1.8 m (6 ft) high and 2.6 m (3½ ft) long.

Another large group of menhirs, the Renaggiu Alignment, stands about half a kilometre (550 yd) away. Starting again from the Stantari menhirs, head south through two fields towards a huge granite outcrop. At its base, shaded by trees, are about 20 large menhirs and many smaller ones. Any sculpted details have long since worn away.

Still more monuments can be found with local advice. Many are scattered across the vineyards on the way to Tizzano, a pretty bay, beach and port with a few holiday homes and, at the end of the road, a drop-outs' camp and caravan site.

BONIFACIO
Harbour, Upper Town, Boat Trips, Beaches

The proud port city of Bonifacio stands on a long, thin peninsula, its high white cliffs of chalk and limestone in striking contrast to the granite of the rest of the island. Towering above a narrow fjord over 1.5 km (1 mile) long, the town is so isolated from the rest of Corsica that the inhabitants speak quite a different dialect. Not so long ago it was easier to get around by sea than by land, and the ports of northern Sardinia, in sight across the straits, are much closer than any in Corsica.

In the 12th century the town was taken by the Genoese, who brought in serfs to run and defend it. Later, when it became a profitable free port under the protection of Genoa, the population stayed of their own free will. Surviving plagues and sieges, Bonifacio preserved its special status until France took over in 1769.

The Harbour

Approaching by land, you first arrive in the lower town around the head of the long inlet, where a few fishing boats and a lot of expensive yachts fill the berths of the Port de Plaisance. Restaurants line the quay along the inlet's south side—and when you would like a change there's another, more varied selection in the Upper Town *(Ville haute)*.

The Port de Commerce is halfway along the inlet, below the cliffs. From March to September, car ferries operate between Bonifacio and Santa Teresa di Gallura in Sardinia. The crossing takes about an hour.

A road from the Port de Plaisance winds its way to the Upper Town but it's far better to go on foot, at least for your first experience. A long steep walk from the port joins the dog-leg of Montée St-Roch, the final approach to the main gate, Porte de Gênes—the only entrance until the mid-19th century.

Col Saint-Roch

The road and footpath divide on the neck of land below the walls. Before you go through the gateway, climb the path opposite, for an extraordinary view of the Upper Town, its houses precariously perched on the edge of the cliff. The Porte de Gênes pierces the huge Bastion de l'Etendard which guards the approach from this direction. Below it, the obtrusive white Chapelle St-Roch marks the spot where the last victim of the 1528 plague died; the epidemic had by then killed off most of the population.

Upper Town

The 16th-century drawbridge and portcullis of the Porte de Gênes, still largely intact, open into Place d'Armes. Where Rue des Deux Empereurs leads off the square, two houses directly opposite each other bear plaques commemorating famous guests. In one dwelling, Charles V, King of Spain and Holy Roman Emperor, spent a short stay in 1541. The other was the home of Napoleon, then a lieutenant-colonel of artillery, from January to March 1793.

In the next street, Rue Palais du Garde, the church of Ste-Marie-Majeure was begun in the 13th century but has since been much altered and restored. Its 14th-century tower is the most elegant feature of the city skyline; the loggia at the west end was added by the Genoese in the 16th century.

Escalier du Roi d'Aragon

Near the 12th-century Torrione tower, 187 steps are cut diagonally into the cliff face from top to bottom. According to legend, they were carved in one night by Spanish forces during a 15th-century siege. Historians dismiss the tale; the steps are older, and the king of Aragon's men failed in any case to take the city by this or any other means. The steps are open on summer afternoons.

Citadel

Parts of the centre and west end of the promontory, the former citadel, are taken up by a military base. Much of the rest is wasteland, neglected since the population declined from its maximum of 8,000 to a few hundred. The Gothic church of St-Dominique, in weathered white limestone, begun in the 13th century, may have been a Templar foundation. If so, it was soon taken over by the Dominicans and became part of a monastery whose other buildings have vanished.

The western tip of the peninsula is still known as Bosco, from the trees that once grew there. Until recently, the few buildings were in ruins, but now the church of St-François and an ancient windmill have been restored.

THE TWO BEST BOAT TRIPS On the west coast near Porto, the lovely **Scandola Peninsula nature reserve** can only be approached by water. And perched on top of high white cliffs, the South's **Bonifacio** is a surreal sight from the sea, and you can combine the trip with a visit to the Lavezzi Islands.

Boat Trips

The best way to appreciate Bonifacio's spectacular location is from the sea; boats leave regularly from the marina to cruise around the cliffs and grottoes. Among the finest sights is the Sdragonata Cave, whose clear blue waters are lit through a "skylight" in the roof shaped just like a map of Corsica. As the boat passes along the southern side of the town, you'll have a good view of the so-called King of Aragon's Staircase.

Iles Lavezzi

Off the coast to the east of Bonifacio is a scattered group of granite islands, rocks and reefs, the remains of the ancient land bridge between Corsica and Sardinia. Excursion boats set out regularly from the marina, taking just over an hour to reach the archipelago. The first of the larger islands, Cavallo, is privately owned and jealously guarded. Landing is forbidden, but it's possible to see where the Romans quarried the silvery, crystalline granite for their palaces and temples; columns are still scattered near the shore.

The rest of the archipelago is a nature reserve, treeless but with several rare plant species that no longer grow in the rest of Corsica. The boats let their passengers off at Lavezzi Island, allotting time for a swim. Hidden reefs in these waters have frequently been fatal to shipping; a graveyard near the landing stage recalls one of the worst disasters, when the *Sémillante*, carrying troops to the Crimean War in 1855, was wrecked and all 773 men on board were drowned.

Beaches

The nearest good beaches of any size are a few kilometres to the east of Bonifacio, facing the Lavezzi Islands. Take the D58 road east and follow signs to Cala Lunga for some of the best.

Plage de la Rondinara

One of the prettiest beaches on this coast, a ring of white sand facing an almost circular bay, lies northeast of Bonifacio. The N198 road to Porto-Vecchio, a fast route through a deserted landscape, passes the surreal sight of the *Amnesia* discothèque, 14 km (9 miles) from town in the middle of nowhere. Just beyond it a sign on the right points to Rondinara. A rough road, but surfaced most of the way, meanders for 7 km (4 miles) through *maquis*, ending at the intensely blue, shallow bay, where a few yachts usually lie at anchor. In summer too many cars compete for the parking space, but the beach is big enough to absorb a crowd and solitude lies only a short walk away.

THE EAST AND CENTRE
Porto-Vecchio, Solenzara, Aléria, Corte, Vallée d'Asco, Castagniccia

Corsica's flat eastern plain, behind its coastline of marsh and sand dunes, was the first choice of early settlers, notably the Romans. Later, when the area proved too difficult to defend against invaders as well as being infested with malaria-carrying mosquitoes, it fell into a long decline. It took modern insecticides and peace to transform it into today's scene of rich farmland, orchards, vineyards and fish farms.

The first rush of tourists ignored the east as being untypical of Corsica, with no rugged peaks, mountain villages or rocky coves. Then ever-increasing numbers of Italians discovered the sandy beaches. Hotels, villas and campsites sprang up and soon other nationalities joined in. After all, the drama of the interior of the island is only a short drive away.

Porto-Vecchio

The holiday business has transformed the Gulf of Porto-Vecchio, part-way up the east coast, from a backwater into one of Corsica's major population centres. Its shores are dotted with an ever-expanding series of resorts, the best being out on the fine sandy beaches of Cala Rossa.

Porto-Vecchio ("old port") has a beautifully sheltered harbour, the best on this coast and important in Roman times. The fortifications on the hill above were built in the 16th century by the Genoese to control the Gulf: today's Genoese and other Italians come in peace (but not quiet) every summer to reclaim it. The port is jammed with pleasure craft and car ferries operate to Livorno and Marseille from July to September. For the rest of the year all reverts to tranquillity.

Inland Excursions

Forests of cork oaks are stripped of their valuable bark every ten years or so, baring a russet-brown trunk until the cork grows back again. Higher up, the cork trees give way to pines, alternating with granite outcrops that grow steeper and become more precipitous until nothing at all can cling to the rock.

The mountain village of L'Ospédale, 20 km (12 miles) from Porto-Vecchio, takes its name from a hospital that stood here centuries ago. Now it's a summer resort, a centre for walks through forests of beech and pine, or more strenuous expeditions to the granite peaks.

Zonza is a pretty village of granite houses, stacked against the hillside with a stunning backdrop of pinnacles, at the junction of four of the most scenic routes in Corsica. Not surprisingly, it attracts hordes of hikers and bikers and enough traffic to jam the narrow streets in July and August. Southwest of Zonza, Levie is the former capital of the Alta Rocca region, with a museum filled with finds from the prehistoric sites in the area. The Castellu de Cucuruzzu, 5 km (3 miles) to the west, is a massive Torréen fortress dating from around 1400 BC.

Col de Bavella

From Zonza northeast to the coast at Solenzara, an ancient Roman road crosses the wild and beautiful Bavella pass. On either side, pinnacles as sharp as needles point skyward out of the pine forest. When Edward Lear published his drawings in 1869 (*Journal of a Landscape Painter in Corsica*) it was assumed that he had exaggerated the vertical scale for dramatic effect; in fact he had recorded it quite faithfully.

Solenzara

A traditional seaside resort, popular with both French and Italian families, Solenzara has a yacht marina, in addition to plenty of camping sites and hotels. A good sandy beach on the north side of town is bordered by groves of sweet-smelling eucalyptus to provide shade, and if the local scenery is unexciting, much more spectacular landscapes are close at hand up the Solenzara river valley.

Aléria

As the only bit of high ground near this stretch of coast, it is clear why the site was settled long ago. It grew even higher as buildings crumbled or were destroyed, and others built on top; walk on it and you will see that you are treading on fragments of ancient brick and pottery.

Greeks and Carthaginians colonized the hill and used the sheltered harbour. Alalia, as it was then known, later became the Roman capital of the island, with a population of about 20,000 – ten times greater than today. In a large fenced area, excavations have revealed temples, baths and an impressive forum. Some of the site has yet to be uncovered.

The Archaeological Museum in the rebuilt Genoese fort has a top-quality collection of discoveries from this and nearby sites, though the labelling is limited, and exhibits from different eras are mixed up together.

Much more recent history was written in 1975, a significant date in the almanac of the nationalist

ALÉRIA

Nestling in the mountain folds of the Corte region, beneath the Popolasca Needles, the white houses of Castiglione.

movement. Just to the north of the modern town, a wine store, Caves Depeille, was occupied by armed members of the movement campaigning for Corsican autonomy. The target was owned by incomers, *pieds-noirs* who had fled from Algeria and were implicated in the adulteration scandals which damaged the reputation of Corsican wines. The protest was quickly crushed by a huge force of police, two of whom died in the resulting gunfight. The burned-out shell of the building can be seen to this day, to the west of the main highway.

Across the road, a track leads down to the Etang de Diane, where the Roman fleet used to anchor. It is now a land-locked salt lake devoted to the raising of oysters, mussels and other shellfish to feed diners all over Corsica. You can try some on the spot; several restaurants line the shore of the lake.

The Road to Corte

From Aléria to Corte, the road alternates between fast modern sections and others where the engineers face a constant battle against landslides. It crosses the River Tavignano by way of a fine Genoese bridge, rebuilt in modern times to take wider vehicles but retaining its handsome lines.

An old chapel, perhaps 11th century, stands close by on the north bank.

Corte

In the very heart of the island, Corte was the cradle of the Corsican independence movement in the 18th century and remains a focus of Corsican nationalism. Its isolation in the past meant that invaders often left it alone. Today it's a popular excursion from all parts of the island, by coach, car or the quaint little train. The University, refounded in 1981, makes study of the Corsican language obligatory; in term time the students inject plenty of life, thronging the streets and bars.

Old Town

The austere Old Town with its sunlit squares stands on a rocky outcrop high above a gorge amid some of the island's most picturesque scenery. Ancient houses with their crumbling arches cling to the rock; dark stairways lead upwards to the citadel perched on the topmost crag.

At the south end of the main street, the Cours Paoli, is the Place Pascal Paoli with a bronze statue of the hero who fought so hard for Corsica's independence. Further up in the Old Town, on the house of his fellow nationalist General Jean-Pierre Gaffori, bullet holes can be seen, a bas-relief on a statue depicts Gaffori's redoubtable wife threatening to blow up the house and everyone within, if anybody attempted to surrender to the Genoese attacks.

Across the road is the Church of the Annunciation where Napoleon's brother Joseph was christened. He was born in a house on the Place du Poilu, to the right of a covered passageway. Near the old bullet-scarred town hall is the restored 18th-century Palais National, originally the Palazzo della Signoria, transformed by Paoli as his seat of government.

A path outside the walls leads to the Belvédère, at the south end of the Citadel, with superb views of the varying greens of vineyards, olive groves and chestnut forests as well as the rugged craters of marble quarries.

Citadel and Museum

Cobblestone steps climb to the gates of the Citadel, the fortress at the summit. Formerly a military barracks, it has taken on a new lease of life. Part has been adapted for use by the University, but much more striking is the new museum (Musée de la Corse), an imaginative blend of old and new by the architect Andrea Bruno. The collections are based on the 3,000 objects accumulated by the ethnologist Father Doazon between 1951 and 1978, but other items are constantly being added.

Labelling is in French and Corsican with an English commentary on cassette.

Minerals, natural history and agriculture are major sections, and an intriguing exhibit on mines and factories goes some way towards answering why almost every industrial enterprise eventually failed. Tourism, the last hope, is traced from its 19th-century beginnings.

An annotated chart of Corsican dialects shows how different even the simplest phrases were from one port to the next. You can listen to traditional Corsican music: polyphonic chants and dances played on instruments both ancient and modern—guitars, violins, banjos and accordions. Amidst a magnificent collection of old prints, books and maps, you walk above a huge reproduction of an all-Corsica map drawn up from a survey undertaken between 1770 and 1795, in spite of the interruptions caused by revolution and war.

Excursions from Corte

The River Tavignano and its tributary the Restonica, which meet at Corte, have cut deep gorges through the mountains. The first is accessible only on foot, like many of the wildest parts of inland Corsica; but the second can be seen by car for much of its length. One problem: the road is inadequate for the demand in high summer (July to mid-September), when it is simply not worth the hassle of having to negotiate the single-track sections only to be confronted by nose-to-tail traffic.

Gorges du Tavignano

Starting below the citadel, you can walk for an hour, a day, or more, following the valley of the Tavignano back into the mountains. About 5 km (3 miles) from Corte, the track enters the gorge itself, sometimes hugging the bank of the fast-flowing river, sometimes climbing high above it. Steep granite cliffs hem in the tree-filled valley on both sides.

Vallée de la Restonica

A road, narrow and bumpy but paved after a fashion, penetrates for 16 km (10 miles) up a steep gorge, winding through pine forest before emerging into a wilderness of sparse *maquis*, surrounded by jagged peaks. It ends with a car park at a height of 1,375 m (4,511 ft), where walkers take to the rocky tracks (signposted) that lead up to two beautiful mountain lakes. Lac de Melo at 1,711 m (5,614 ft) is an hour's march away, by way of some steep scrambles; Lac de Capitello, at 1,930 m (6,332 ft), is a further 40 minutes' walk by a rough path.

Vallée d'Asco

From the road and rail junction of Ponte Leccia, a turning off the main highway to Calvi heads west up the magnificent gorge of the River Asco. Only constructed in modern times, the road is an engineering masterpiece and unusually well-surfaced, but still needs to be treated with normal caution. Cut into the side of the V-shaped river valley it passes the town of Asco and then twists its way higher and higher, every bend revealing more breathtaking views. Cattle, mules and donkeys wander along the road, and beehives dot the hillsides; Asco honey, on sale in the town, is famous for its flavour.

The river tumbles over rocks, among pine and birch trees, with massive peaks and sharp ridges on every side. A stroll in the forest might yield a glimpse of some wild sheep, deer or boar. The end of the road, Hauts d'Asco, was built as a ski centre, but snow is not frequent, heavy or predictable enough to support a ski resort anywhere in Corsica, even on the slopes of its highest mountain.

Castagniccia

The hilly region between Corte and the east coast takes its name from the chestnut trees *(castagno)* which were planted in huge numbers by the Genoese. Dried and ground into flour, the nuts became the staple diet of inland Corsica. The Castagniccia was where the trees grew best, and it supported a large population. With the advent of cheap wheat flour, the forests were neglected, and emigration has left the pretty villages, clinging to hillsides or perched on mountain ridges, largely deserted. The area is served by a network of narrow roads, winding through the still beautiful woods. In autumn, all turns to gold and wild boars gorge on the fallen chestnuts.

Morosaglia

On the western edge of the Castagniccia, Morosaglia's claim to fame is as the birthplace of the patriot Pascal Paoli. The house where he was born in 1725 is now a museum. In 1889, his remains were brought from England, where he had been buried in 1807, and reinterred in the basement chapel.

Cervione

The largest of the region's villages and easily reached from the east coast, Cervione actually has a cathedral. It was established when a bishop moved his seat inland from Aléria to escape the malarial mosquitoes. The Bishop's Palace was used by the "King" of Corsica, the adventurer Theodor von Neuhoff, during his brief reign in 1736.

THE NORTHEAST
Bastia, Cap Corse, Saint-Florent, Le Nebbio

The northeast includes as much variety as any other part of the island, contrasting scrubland and forgotten Pisan churches with the traffic jams and fumes of Bastia, Corsica's biggest city. Cap Corse, the peninsula forming the northern extremity, offers some rugged stretches of coast and a wild interior. A tour right round this finger of land could start and finish at Bastia or Saint-Florent, set on a lovely bay on the cape's western base.

Bastia

Corsica's major port and industrial hub was the island's capital during Genoese rule; it is now the administrative centre of the *département* of Haute-Corse. A tough town with Chicago-style politics, Bastia has also spearheaded the island's perennial independence movement. It looks more Italian than French; tall, flat-roofed houses rise in terraces up the hillside, forming a theatre best viewed from the sea.

The walled citadel (also called Terra Nova) stands high above the Old Port (Vieux Port) and Old Town (Terra Vecchia). To the north lies the New Port (Nouveau Port) with, just inland, the main commercial area and shopping streets. North again are some prosperous suburbs and the road to Cap Corse.

Citadel

The well-preserved 15th-century citadel, with its impressive tower and ramparts, dates from the Genoese occupation. A drawbridge leads to the former Governor's Palace, now housing the Corsican Ethnological Museum on its lower floors. The museum is in the throes of a long-term, much needed reorganization, but you can expect to see Roman and other archaeological relics, souvenirs of famous Corsican personalities and displays of the island's traditional crafts and customs.

Nearby are the two baroque churches of Ste-Marie, with ancient tombs and a richly decorated altar, and Ste-Croix, named for its crucifix which fishermen supposedly found floating in the sea on a pool of light.

Old Port and Old Town

To the north below the citadel, the Old Port is the preserve of pleasure craft and a few fishing boats that spread their sails and

The church of St-Jean Baptiste stands proud above the old port.

nets out to dry in the sun. It offers a better selection of restaurants in a small area than anywhere else in Bastia.

Also facing the harbour is the tall façade of the baroque church of St-Jean-Baptiste. The city's largest, it has two splendid towers but a rather depressing interior, apart from an ornate altar of multi-coloured Corsican marble.

Behind the church is a maze of narrow alleys and steep stairways, bordered by multi-storey tenement houses of the 16th and 17th centuries. The large Place de l'Hôtel de Ville functions as a market square on weekday mornings, although surprisingly few stalls set up for business.

Rue Napoléon runs north from the Old Town towards the newer commercial areas, past the 17th-century Oratory of the Immaculate Conception. The interior of the church is rather like a jewel box, lined with damask and rich dark wood. It was used for meetings of the assembly convened under the short-lived Anglo-Corsican alliance of the mid-1790s.

New Port
The heart of the modern city is the long esplanade of Place St-Nicolas, open on one side to the quay where giant car ferries dock, watched by a statue of Napoleon as emperor. Some of the earthy spirit of traditional Corsica can be sensed in the area's smoky bars or in the banter to be heard over the click of the *boules* under the plane and palm trees. Parallel to Place St-Nicolas is the fashionable shopping street, Boulevard Paoli.

South of Bastia
An expressway dives through a tunnel from the New Port, under the Old Port and the citadel, and emerges into a zone of flat land and ugly commercial development that stretches all the way to the airport, 23 km (14 miles) to the south. Mixed in with it are a number of hotels (the city itself is surprisingly short of them), including one or two of the chain variety so familiar on the French mainland but otherwise absent from Corsica.

THE THREE FINEST PISAN CHURCHES The Romanesque basilicas built by the Pisans are the architectural jewels of Corsica. Among the best are **La Canonica** south of Bastia; **Santa Maria Assunta**, the "Cathedral of the Nebbio" at Saint-Florent; and in the hills inland, **San Michele** at Murato.

La Marana

An alternative route from Bastia to its airport follows a long, narrow strip of reclaimed swamp and sand dunes, divided from the mainland by a huge lagoon bordered by reed beds, the Etang de Biguglia.

Closed communities of holiday homes restrict access to the sea, but tracks cut through the littoral to it at several points, mainly near the southern end—the sandy beaches are equipped with bars, cafés and windsurfers for rent.

Mariana and La Canonica

Near the airport is the site of the Roman settlement of Mariana, abandoned in the 10th century when it became impossible to defend against raiders from the sea. Scattered ruins, the foundations of houses, baths and early Christian churches, are difficult to interpret; the highlight is a mosaic floor decorated with a bearded Neptune surrounded by dolphins and other sea creatures.

The Pisans attempted to revive the Christian community here in the 12th century. La Canonica, their church in basilica form with an apse at the east end, is a marvel of elegance and restrained decoration. Standing alone in the flat landscape, the structure has recently been beautifully restored; the interior has been left plain.

Cap Corse

The northern tip of the island may not look very large on the map, and it is a mere 40 km (25 miles) long, but don't imagine it to be a short excursion, a matter of two or three hours. If you plan to drive right round it, you should allow most of a day—and the rest to recover. The full circuit is quite a test of stamina for drivers and passengers, and anyone likely to suffer from car-sickness should give it a miss. A much better plan would be to stay overnight along the way and enjoy some of the scenic diversions.

If you have a choice, think about which direction you want to take around the cape. Heading up the east coast and down the west means you have the best sea views, and easier access to scenic parking spots, but you are closer to the edge on the more verti-ginous sections. Before the road was built, the only access was by sea, and Cap Corse bred the island's best sailors. A boat trip is still a great way to see it.

Lavasina

North along the coast road from Bastia is the pilgrimage town of Lavasina. In the church of Notre-Dame-des-Grâces, the devout pay homage to a 16th-century portrait of the Virgin and Child (above the altar) believed to have the miraculous power to save sailors

CAP CORSE

and fishermen in peril at sea. The biggest crowds come on 7th September for a procession on the beach, and the following day, the Virgin's birthday.

Erbalunga

The next fishing village to the north is a favourite with painters and photographers. Colourful old houses clustered round its rocky harbour are packed so tightly that they appear to grow out of the sea. At the entrance stands one of many Genoese lookout towers built along this coast to warn of the approach of pirates.

Marine-de-Sisco

A little fishing village with a couple of hotels and restaurants stands where the River Sisco reaches the sea. Inland, 8 km (5 miles) up its valley, is a cluster of hamlets, Chioso being the largest. Reached by a rocky track (signposted) is San Michele, a handsome little 11th-century Romanesque chapel built by the Pisans. Back at the coast Santa Catalina's church used to house a collection of holy relics, attracting crowds of pilgrims. They were kept in its round crypt, but are no longer on view.

The speckled church of San Michele de Murato. The belltower was an afterthought.

Macinaggio

Further up the peninsula the heather-covered landscape grows wilder; it comes as a surprise to find a large yacht marina. There has long been a port here; it welcomed Paoli on his return from his English exile in 1790, and Napoleon put in when fleeing from Paoli's supporters in 1793. The coast to the north is a nature reserve, rich in birdlife and with beautiful coastal walks.

The road turns inland and climbs to Rogliano on Mont Poggio, with a bird's-eye view over much of the northern cape. Further west, at Col de Serra, a short walk leads to Moulin Mattei, a restored windmill commanding a panorama of the peninsula's mountains and west coast.

Centuri-Port

Set on the west coast of Cap Corse, Centuri-Port is a favourite base for diving and fishing. Tiled houses with roofs of green slate surround the harbour and several hotels and restaurants cater to the steady stream of summer visitors arriving by land and sea.

Nonza

South of Centuri-Port, the mountains meet the sea in a coastline of steep cliffs and rocky coves. The medieval fortified town of Nonza perches on a clifftop, with a massive lookout tower rising above its stone-roofed houses. In the 16th-century church, an altar painting portrays St Julia, the island's patron saint who was martyred here for rejecting the local pagan cult.

Saint-Florent

Reclining in the arms of its magnificent bay at the base of Cap Corse, the present-day resort and port grew out of the little town which clustered for protection around the great circular Genoese fortress and citadel. Houses and hotels in pretty pastel shades face the yachting harbour and there are two good beaches, though weed tends to gather on the eastern stretches.

The vineyards inland are famous for their muscat grapes and the wines of the Patrimonio *appellation* are sold in the town and especially in Patrimonio itself, just up the road on the way to Bastia. At the top of the Col de Teghime, a pass above Bastia, a memorial honours French-led Berber troops from North Africa who died in the 1943 liberation campaign.

Santa Maria Assunta

The church called the "cathedral of the Nebbio" stands just outside Saint-Florent, east of the main square along Rue Giustiniani. Perfect in its simplicity and restrained decoration, it is one of the best of the many Romanesque churches built by the Pisans in the north of the island. This one dates from the 13th century and has been beautifully restored. Mummified remains in a glass case inside are said to be those of St Flor, a Roman soldier martyred in the 3rd century.

Le Nebbio

South of Saint-Florent is a region of deep, green valleys hemmed in by an arc of steep hills. Strung round it like a necklace, villages cling to the upper slopes and summits, their churches and bell-towers standing out above olive groves, woods and pastures.

Oletta

Appearing to hang on a near-vertical hillside, Oletta is a village of tall fortress-like houses. Many were originally built with no entrance at ground level, and some doors still have to be reached by stairs. The main square is like a balcony over the valley; the 18th-century church facing it has a much more ancient bas-relief stone-carving set into its wall. Inside is a triptych painted in 1534, with a central panel of the Virgin and Child.

Murato

Passing shepherds' stone huts, the road climbs to the top of a grassy escarpment, looking down on soaring sparrowhawks and kites. Before reaching the village you'll come to an eye-catching 13th-century Pisan church, San Michele, built of pale marble and dark-green serpentine. Its classic lines are marred by a later belltower, in which the stonemasons didn't bother to preserve the balance of dark and light stone.

Western Nebbio

Every Nebbio village seems to have some strange or unique feature. The houses of Rapale, built of grey schist, are like miniature castles. At Pieve, three prehistoric menhirs are set into a stone platform in front of the belltower. In Sorio look for a sign indicating *Monument Historique à 150 m*, down a steep track just east of the tall belltower. Hidden among oak trees is a tiny Pisan church, with a recently restored roof. The interior is empty apart from an elaborate altar, from a later period.

Santo Pietro di Tenda has twin baroque churches adjoining a shared belltower. Their upkeep is evidently too great a burden for the village and they are falling into a decrepit state. The one still in use and occasionally open, Eglise St-Jean, has an elaborate *trompe l'œil* interior simulating rich marble.

Désert des Agriates

West of Saint-Florent the D81 road leaves the coast to cut through a land of granite outcrops, tumbled rocks and patches of scrub and cactus. Its name, roughly translated as "desert of farms", seems an odd contradiction until you realize that it was once productive, until overgrazing, fires and soil erosion took their toll.

The north coast, reached by only a few tracks, has some lovely beaches, in particular Saleccia, a long stretch of sand, and Loto, a sheltered cove.

The Genoese tower at Punta di Mortella gave its name, with vowels transposed, to the Martello towers built much later round the coast of the British Isles.

4

THE FOUR BEST MUSEUMS The **Musée de la Préhistoire** at Sartène evokes the mysteries of the distant past; **Aléria's museum** displays remarkable finds from the classical era; the modern **Musée de la Corse** at Corte covers Corsican culture and recent history; and the **Fesch Museum of Art** in Ajaccio has some superb Old Master paintings.

THE NORTH-WEST
L'Ile-Rousse, Algajola, Calvi, Calenzana, Galéria

Northwest Corsica includes the fertile and populous Haute-Balagne region, the hinterland of its main ports of Calvi and L'Ile-Rousse. By contrast the coast and interior southwest of Calvi is virtually a desert, depopulated since the 16th century when North African pirates carried off many of its people to serve as slaves and the rest fled to safer areas.

L'Ile-Rousse

Jutting out into the sea in the centre of the northwest coast is an attractive town and port founded by Paoli himself in the 18th century. The great nationalist wanted to create an outlet for exporting the Balagne's olive oil, wine and honey.

Facing Place Paoli, the large central square, is a covered market built like a Greek temple. The square and the streets leading to the port are lined with dozens of restaurants. On summer evenings vacationers wander around, comparing the menus and prices displayed before choosing where to dine. Frequent ferries from Nice and Marseille discharge hundreds of summer visitors every day. A safe, gently sloping sandy beach right next to town attracts families. Water-skiers and a sailing school take advantage of the sheltered bay next to the port.

The "red isle" that gave the town its name is connected to the mainland by a causeway, allowing a pleasant sunset stroll past the ferry terminal and up to the top of the red granite hill. L'Ile-Rousse is protected from the prevailing winds, and the season seems longer here than elsewhere on the coast, but by the end of October all is quiet.

Algajola

Reached by a short diversion off the main coastal highway, Algajola comprises a Genoese citadel, a single road running parallel to a lovely beach, and a handful of modest hotels and restaurants. The little train connecting Calvi and L'Ile-Rousse passes through two or three times a day. It all adds up to an agreeable small resort, quieter than its two big neighbours but within easy reach of them, as well as the scenic countryside and villages of the Haute-Balagne.

Aregno

Although the beach at Algajola calls itself Aregno-Plage, the vil-

Speloncato makes an interesting stop on the Route des Artisans.

lage of Aregno is up in the nearby hills, about 15 km (9 miles) away by road. Its 12th-century church of La Trinità is a showpiece of multicoloured stone: shades of green, yellow, orange and brown arranged in a dazzling pattern. With sculpture and unusually elaborate carved decoration, it's one of the finest examples of Pisan Romanesque.

LA ROUTE DES ARTISANS

Signs all along the north coast between L'Ile-Rousse and Calvi suggest a diversion to see some picturesque villages and their crafts. With official encouragement, many traditional techniques have been preserved, or revived where they had died out. Young people have been given grants to establish potteries, blacksmiths' forges, leather and furniture workshops. And the increase in tourist traffic has spurred olive oil producers, winemakers, beekeepers and bakers into setting up shops and displays along the way.

The *Route des Artisans* is not just one, but a network of narrow mountain roads through the Haute-Balagne, from Palasca in the east to Calenzana in the west. Between them, Belgodere, Speloncato, Feliceto, Cateri, Pigna and Corbara are all worth a stop.

Sant' Antonino

One of the oldest and most picturesque villages in Corsica has become a magnet for summer visitors. Some of its houses are available for holiday rental, and for those staying down at the coast, Sant' Antonino is a popular spot to include in an excursion. Its streets are too steep and narrow for cars; you park below the village and walk up to find its small shops selling local products and the two or three restaurants that serve traditional dishes.

Calvi

The two-level town of Calvi curves seductively around a bay. The imposing citadel stands on a rocky promontory, high above the port and marina, a fashionable sailing centre packed with craft of all sizes. The high dome of Ste-Marie-Majeure church dominates the lower town. It was founded in the 4th century, probably on the site of a Roman temple, but the present building dates from the 18th century and the belltower from the 19th. A wooden sculpture and two paintings of the Madonna are among its treasures.

The golden sand beaches east of the port are a major attraction—the main stretch is 6 km (4 miles) long. There are grottoes to be explored and, inland, a range of mountain walks limited only by your energy and time.

Upper Town

The shady alleys inside the old citadel make a change from the sun-baked beaches. Reached from Place Christophe-Colomb, the massive granite ramparts were built by the Genoese in the 15th century when Calvi was the region's main port.

The 13th-century church of St-Jean-Baptiste, often restored, is noted for its crucifix and other woodcarvings, multi-coloured marble altar and alabaster font adorned with the arms of 14th-century Calvi families. It faces the Place d'Armes with its handsome houses, including the former Genoese governor's palace, a 13th-century building which has been used by the Foreign Legion.

Accepting that Christopher Columbus was of Genoese stock, some of the locals insist that he was actually born in Calvi, even identifying one of the houses on Rue Colombo as his birthplace. Historians are unconvinced. But there is no dispute about the connection with Admiral Lord Nelson (then a captain), who lost an eye during the British naval siege of 1793.

Calenzana

In the hills 14 km (9 miles) southeast of Calvi, Calenzana is the centre of a prosperous area planted with vineyards, orchards, olive groves and market gardens. It stands on the lower slopes of Monte Grosso, and is the starting point of the longest of Corsica's marked trails, the GR20. Crossing the mountains and ending in the southeast corner of the island, it takes even the fittest of hikers about 12 days.

An inscription on the belltower records the death in 1732 of "five hundred Germans", soldiers hired by the Genoese to put down a rebellion. According to legend, the people of Calenzana threw beehives down at the invaders from their upper windows. The Germans, maddened by multiple stings, were then easily overcome.

The church of Santa Restituta is a pilgrimage site honouring a local martyr, executed in 303. Her marble sarcophagus dates from later in the 4th century.

Galéria

The only sizeable settlement on the wild and deserted coast south of Calvi, Galéria sits in splendid isolation between red rocks and a turquoise sea and has recently acquired a handful of hotels, villas and hostels. For walkers it can be the beginning (or end) of trails across the island or down its west side. Divers come for the clear water, sailors for the beautiful bays all around. The main beach is sheltered and sandy; another to the north is a favourite of nudists.

CULTURAL NOTES

Dream Hunters

In an island of myths and legends none is more powerful or more widely believed than that of the *mazzeri*, or dream hunters. In or out of their bodies, they are said to leave their sleeping spouses at night and go after wild boar or smaller animals with their knives, sticks or bare hands. At the moment of the kill, they may see in the face of their prey the features of a relative or friend. And when they do, that person will die within a year. Dorothy Carrington, author of *The Granite Island* and *The Dream Hunters of Corsica*, reported meeting an old man who had dreamt he had killed a boar, and seen the face of his nephew in Marseille; the news of the nephew's death soon followed.

In the old days the *mazzeri*, men or women, would name the people they had seen, in what amounted to a curse. They acquired a status akin to witches, although they were not blamed for the deaths they foretold. People claimed to have seen them wandering around at night at times when they were known to be asleep in their beds, and some were credited with the power of transforming themselves into fierce dogs.

The *mazzeri* may be a relic of the pre-Christian era, but most Corsicans still believe in their existence today.

Music

You'll gain some idea of the great range of Corsican music by listening to recordings in the sound booths at the Musée de la Corse in Corte, or some of the hundreds of CDs and tapes available in the shops. Best of all, go to a concert by today's performers. Until recent times, little was written down, let alone recorded. Folk songs, hymns and *voceri*—calls for vengeance sung by a woman—were handed down over the centuries by oral tradition. Folk enthusiasts brought some of the songs and chants to a wider public in the 19th century, but only when it began to be associated with the modern nationalist movement did Corsican music really take off.

Les Nouvelles Polyphonies Corses, a quintet of singers, have adapted the haunting polyphonic choral music of Corsica for an international audience. So have the five women of the group Donnisulana, whose unaccompanied voices combine in thrilling harmony, whether they are singing old madrigals, modern feminist songs or nationalist anthems. Even more overtly political are groups such as I Chjami Aghjalesi, or the veteran performers I Muvrini, who were actually banned from appearing for a few years in the late-1970s for inflaming nationalist passions. These days, they can fill any venue in Bastia—or Paris.

CULTURAL NOTES

Sign Language
Every town and village has a "French" name (actually in most cases Italian, inherited from the period of Genoese rule) and a Corsican name. They are rarely the same, though the difference may be as little as a 'u' for an 'o', as in Murato and Vergio which are Muratu and Verghiu in Corsican. Aiacciu is recognizable as Ajaccio, but other changes can be more radical: Saint-Florent is San Fiurenzu in Corsican, and Propriano becomes P'upria. Old signposts may give only the French version, which local campaigners will often amend into Corsican, or paint over completely. For the last 20 years or so, new signs have shown both names, but the more extreme language liberationists may still delete the one they think of as French.

Trail Blazers
In 1765, the young James Boswell, friend and later biographer of Dr Samuel Johnson, came to pay homage to "a people actually fighting for liberty" and their leader Pascal Paoli. So impressed was he by Paoli and his cause that on returning to London, he called on the Prime Minister (Pitt the Elder) to urge him to lend support, even if it meant war with France. He published *An Account of Corsica, the Journal of a Tour to that Island* and *Memoirs of Pascal Paoli* (1768), classics of early travel writing.

Prosper Mérimée came to France's newly acquired province as an Inspector of Historic Monuments, touring the island on horseback in 1840 in search of ancient sites. He was equally fascinated by the concept of *vendetta*. This never-ending blood feud is quintessentially Corsican, and a famous example caught his imagination. The result was his novel *Colomba*, the account of a village split into two factions by old enmities and recent murders. In Mérimée's version, a young man returns after years abroad to find that he is expected to avenge the latest killing. Colomba, his sister, manipulates events so that he is drawn into the conflict against his will and forced to kill in self-defence.

Alexandre Dumas stayed in the castle at Sollacaro that had once sheltered Pasca Paoli, and produced a blood-and-thunder adventure, *Les Frères Corses*.

Guy de Maupassant's tales on themes of love, vendetta and banditry are as much a hymn to the scenic beauties of the island as to its customs.

As a young man, Gustave Flaubert toured Corsica and wrote an evocative travel journal, *Memoires d'un Fou*.

Alphonse Daudet's visit included a landing on the Lavezzi Islands where hundreds of soldiers drowned when their ship was wrecked in 1855. His *Lettres de Mon Moulin* evoke the lonely life of Corsica's lighthouse keepers.

Shopping

Local arts and crafts are flourishing. Often with state support, workshops for glass and pottery, metalwork, woodcarving and basketry have been set up in many mountain villages.

The Essentials
For basic supplies—picnic food, toiletries and beachwear for example—you can't beat the selection or the prices at the hypermarkets on the outskirts of Ajaccio, Bastia and Calvi. Everything is more expensive and the choice much more limited in smaller resorts and village shops.

Crafts and Souvenirs
A range of craft goods is on sale in city shops, but it's more fun to trace their source. The tourist offices will point you in the right direction. The villages of Haute-Balagne in the north of the island have been especially publicized, but people are beginning to catch on in all the mountain areas, starting up little shops to sell local products.

The texture and unusual patterns of olive wood are turned to advantage in salad bowls, and chestnut is traditionally used for furniture. Charming music boxes carved from wood are painted to depict figures in Corsican folk costume. The most skilled among the woodworkers are the makers of musical instruments—guitars, mandolins and spinets.

Large pieces of cork are made into fruit bowls and mats, and off-cuts bonded together to make effective wine-coolers. Some of the island's many potteries have revived prehistoric designs, others produce more delicate ceramics with subtle glazes. Handmade glassware includes lamps and flagons, or decorative objects such as vases. Rugs and soft toys are made from sheepskin, and dolls are dressed in miniature versions of woven or embroidered regional costume.

It's hard to avoid souvenirs of Napoleon here on his native island. Busts in every conceivable material, tea towels, T-shirts and mugs all carry the image of the emperor. But seen even more frequently is the profile of an African head, which has been adopted by the nationalist movement.

CDs and Cassettes
You may have found your foot tapping to the rhythms of Corsican folk-rock, often associated with the independence movement

and played in many bars and restaurants. Or perhaps the haunting *a cappella* chants of ancient airs have caught your ear. If so, you can take home a recorded reminder. Many shops and market stalls have a small selection of CDs and cassettes, but the best stock in the island is at Planète, on Boulevard Paoli in Bastia.

Food and Drink
Depending on the import restrictions in your home country, you might like to carry back some of the local *charcuterie*. The smoked mountain hams are especially good, and can be found in convenient vacuum packs If you have developed a taste for any of the Corsican cheeses, they too would make a short-lived memento. And don't forget a pot of the famous mountain honey, for example from Asco.

Wine tasting is offered right next to the vineyards or in the villages of all the winegrowing regions. If you have your own vehicle and will be returning to another EU country, you can carry as much as you want (for your own use) and as space allows. But beware: it's all too easy to buy too much and pay too much for very ordinary wine, especially after you have been plied with glass after glass of free samples by friendly producers in a beautiful setting. Try to gain some experience of a selection of wines, and compare with supermarket prices, before stocking up. Corsica also makes its own special liqueurs flavoured with wild herbs and fruits.

THE MOOR'S HEAD

The silhouette of a young man's head, in black with a white bandana tied around his brow, was used by Paoli's supporters in the 18th century as a symbol of independence. Before that, it appeared on the coins issued during the brief reign of "King" Theodor von Neuhoff, but it had been associated with Corsica even earlier. The head featured on the banners of the Aragonese kings who long coveted the island, probably in commemoration of their defeat of the Moors (also known as Saracens) who had once occupied most of Spain. Corsicans took it as their own after a legendary victory over a Saracen army. The story goes that the invaders were pursuing the Corsican folk hero Paoli (not the later leader) who had rescued a Christian girl from the Moorish stronghold of Granada. These days, the Moor's Head is displayed by nationalists on anything from cars to the banners held aloft at concerts by their favourite group, I Muvrini.

Sports

The turquoise sea is infinitely tempting, and most visitors head straight for it to swim, snorkel, sail or windsurf. But many others come to Corsica to walk.

Water Sports

A beach is never far away. The west and northwest have plenty of sheltered bays and coves with limpid blue water; the long east coast is an almost continuous stretch of sand, although the sea may not be as clean. At popular beaches, you'll find boats and sailboards to hire by the hour, and conditions to suit most levels of skill. The bigger resorts have sailing schools with flotillas of small dinghies for children and absolute beginners, and catamarans for the more advanced classes.

Take your snorkel and flippers, or buy a set of gear when you arrive. Except after a storm, the sea is wonderfully clear and there are plenty of colourful fish. Scuba-diving clubs all around the coast offer classes to gain the necessary qualifications, and have equipment for rent.

You can fish in the rivers—tourist offices can tell you about rules and locations—and the sea. Ask at the big yacht marinas if you want to hire a boat by the day or half-day to go sport-fishing offshore. Canoeing or rafting down the fast-flowing rivers is best in spring when water levels are high.

On Land

Larger hotels may have their own tennis courts; if not, tourist offices can direct you to local courts. Golfers will find a scattering of courses, for example at Lumio on the north coast and Spérone near Bonifacio, a championship course created by top designer Robert Trent Jones.

Bicycles can be hired at most resorts; mountain bikes too, and you'll be grateful for the low gears when you start to climb away from the coast. The many equestrian centres offer pony-trekking along the coasts and in the mountains.

Walks and Treks

A network of over 1,000 km (620 miles) of marked hiking trails has been established, crossing the island by way of mountain peaks, forests, river valleys and gorges. Cabins have been built to provide overnight shelter where the route is far from any village.

SPORTS

The best-known of the trails is the GR20, part of the French system of *Sentiers de Grande Randonnée* (long-distance footpaths designated by the French walkers' federation, the FFRP). Starting from Calenzana in the northwest, it runs for 200 km (125 miles) to Conca in the southeast, and can take up to 15 days to complete, depending on fitness levels and side excursions. Other paths, maintained like the GR20 by the Regional Natural Park authorities, include three from the east to the west coast, the *Mare a Mare Nord, Centre* and *Sud*. Crossing the mountains of the north, centre and south respectively, each of these can take over a week.

It's essential to be well prepared and equipped if you are going to undertake one of these expeditions. That means having the right footwear and clothing for all weathers, a compass, detailed maps (even though the routes are marked with colour-coded blazes), and the Topo-Guide for the route published by the FFRP. Unauthorized camping *(camping sauvage)* is forbidden because of the fire risk. That, and the existence of refuges and other accommodation with optional meals along the way, means you don't have to carry heavy packs, but you'll need food and water for at least a day.

All the routes involve innumerable steep climbs and descents; you need to be in good shape to start and with luck you'll be even fitter at the end. Keep an eye on the weather and try to get a forecast whenever you can.

You can always walk just part of one of the main trails, or one of countless other paths that take just an hour or two. A golden rule: don't take short cuts through the *maquis*. If there is meant to be a path, there will be one. What might look like a quick way down to the sea could lead over a precipice, and at best you'll be faced with a long slog back to the path you ill-advisedly left.

Spectator Sports

Almost any evening, local men can be seen enjoying a game of *boules* in dusty town squares. The other national passion is soccer. Every town has its team but Bastia's competes in France's premier league and often beats the best from the mainland.

Real experts show how to drive the mountain roads in the Tour de Corse rally in May, and there are frequent cycle races. Calvi holds an October "Festival of the Wind" in which every sort of airborne sport or vaguely wind-related transport is represented: balloonists, paragliders and microlight pilots come from all over Europe.

Dining Out

Although strongly influenced by France and Italy—judging from cafés in the resorts you could be forgiven for thinking that pizza is the national dish—Corsican cuisine has a personality all its own. Many local dishes are based on the island's particular resources: the sea, the herds of goats and semi-wild boars, the wild herbs and the sweet chestnut.

Where?

In the resorts and larger towns, great numbers of restaurants compete for your custom, offering typical French or Italian cooking, Corsican dishes or international fast food. Mountain villages may have only one or two eating places (and they may close in winter). Prices are reasonable, especially if you stick to the set menus.

Local Flavours

The abundant wildlife of the *maquis* is turned into a variety of tasty preparations seasoned with herbs—try wild boar *(sanglier)* in the form of a terrine or *daube* (stew). *Soupe corse* is a rich and filling mixture of red beans and garlic, odd bits of *charcuterie* and other meats; it can almost make a meal in itself.

Pigs fed on chestnuts and goats that graze the *maquis* would seem to season themselves. Cuts of pork are then cured and smoked to produce the robust hams for which Corsica is famous. An *assiette de charcuterie*, a plateful of such delicacies, can be as good as you'll find anywhere. *Figatelli* is a peppery pork liver sausage.

Lamb *(agnellu)* and pork *(porcu)* come roasted, grilled or in rich stews *(tianu)*. Wild boar or kid can be roasted over an open fire scented with herbs, or simmered in red wine. *Stuffatu* (lamb or kid with onions and noodles), *cabrettu à l'istretta* (stewed kid with spices) and *tianu di fave* (pork with broad beans) are other succulent choices. Different areas have their own dishes, such as Bonifacio's stuffed aubergines.

All this concentration on meat means that vegetarians have practically no choice and may have to depend on salads and pasta.

Fish and Seafood

Quayside restaurants in every port and fishing village display freshly caught fish as well as

Dining Out

Take a seat in one of Calvi's harbourside restaurants and indulge in a fresh fish dinner.

locally farmed oysters and mussels for an on-the-spot selection. Spiny lobster *(langouste)* is grilled or served with a local version of mayonnaise; *moules marinière* are mussels lightly cooked in white wine with onions or shallots, herbs and cream. The Mediterranean fish such as *daurade* (bream) and *loup de mer* (sea bass) are excellent grilled with fennel. *Aziminu* is a Corsican version of *bouillabaisse*, the filling stew of fish and shellfish for which Marseille is famous. This and the piquant *soupe de poissons* are both accompanied by fresh bread spread with *rouille*, spicy garlic mayonnaise, and sprinkled with grated cheese. Wild trout caught in mountain rivers make the farmed variety taste bland.

Cheeses

Corsica is famous for its cheeses made from the milk of goats *(fromage de chèvre)* and ewes *(de brebis)*. At their best between autumn and spring, some of the ewe's-milk cheeses are sent to mainland France to mature in the caves of Roquefort and develop into the sharp blue cheese of that name. Local people like to eat ewe's-milk cheeses with sweet white grapes. The fresh, white *brocciu* is a mild, soft goat's cheese used in many pasta dishes.

Desserts

The typical fixed-price *menu* tends to offer a limited choice: mousse au chocolat, *crème caramel*, ice creams or sorbets. But in restaurants featuring Corsican cooking, you may find rustic delicacies based on the old-time staple, the sweet chestnut. Although the mountain forests are not as extensive as they once were, the nuts are still gathered by spreading huge nets under the most productive trees in October to catch the falling crop. The flour made from ground chestnuts (which can be used for bread) goes into the making of delicate, crisp *fritelle* (fritters) and *pisticcini* (tartlets). Chestnut purée *(crème de marrons)* with creamy *brocciu* cheese is a delicious combination.

Drinks

All the requirements for wine-growing are in place: Mediterranean sunshine, hillsides where breezes cool the air, the right soil (not too rich) and a tradition of viticulture stretching back to pre-Roman times. It is only surprising that Corsican wines have never made a name for themselves outside France and are still mainly appreciated in the island itself. Past scandals set them back—the illegal addition of sugar and various adulterants actually led to the first real violence in the present nationalist campaign.

Sweet white wine from muscat grapes is a local favourite, before dinner or with dessert. Much of the drier white wine is from the distinctive *vermentinu* grape, and red from the aromatic *sciacarellu*. Strong and full-bodied, the latter was used in the past to bolster thinner wines from the mainland. A lot of rosé is produced—it goes down well with menus of fish or meat, and seems to suit the summer atmosphere of eating at open-air tables.

In restaurants, the house wines, by *pichet* (jug) or *demi* (half-litre) are generally reliable, but for a few francs more you can try the regional *appélations* such as Patrimonio from near Saint-Florent, Calvi or Porto-Vecchio.

Typically Corsican apéritifs are made from wine and herbs— the regulars in the bars generally order an aniseed-flavoured *pastis* diluted with ice-cold water. There's a fiery local brandy, and various *eaux-de-vie* are distilled from the wines and flavoured with lemon or myrtle berries.

Beer is brewed on the island, but all the usual international brands are imported as well. And of course there's no shortage of fruit juices, mineral waters and soft drinks.

Coffee comes Italian-style, as a small espresso, unless you specify a double, or with milk *(café au lait)*.

The Hard Facts

To help you plan your trip, here are some of the practical details you should know about Corsica.

Airports

Ajaccio's Campo dell'Oro airport is 7 km (4 miles) from the city. Buses run to the centre (SNCF station) throughout the day, taking about 20 minutes. Bastia airport (Poretta) is 23 km (14 miles) south of the city; Calvi's Sainte Catherine airport lies 7 km (4 miles) southeast of town; and Figari airport is 24 km (15 miles) southwest of Porto-Vecchio (and slightly closer to Bonifacio). Buses and taxis are available.

All four main airports have daily non-stop services to and from Paris, Marseille and other French cities, with connections to the rest of Europe. They are served by many charter flights from the UK and other European cities in summer, fewer in spring and autumn and scarcely any in winter.

Car Rental

Hiring a car is a convenient way of getting around, although rates are quite high by comparison with other holiday destinations. Some major international companies are represented in Corsica, and it may be worth making a reservation through one of them in your home country before your visit. Good local companies also operate from the airports, cities and resorts, but whichever you use, check that rates include full insurance against loss and damage, and local taxes. There is usually no limit on the distance you can cover, but an extra charge may be levied for drop-off at a different location, and for additional driver(s).

To rent a car, you need to be over 21 (25 with some companies) and have a current driving licence. You are expected to pay with a major credit card, which will save you having to leave a large cash deposit.

Climate

Summers are hot and dry, with day temperatures often over 30°C (86°F) on the coast, tempered by sea breezes. Inland it can be much cooler, particularly at night. Winters are mild, with occasional rain, especially in the mountains where snow sometimes falls at higher altitudes. Spring and au-

THE HARD FACTS

tumn are changeable but most days are pleasantly warm and sunny.

Clothing

Take lightweight clothing in summer (cotton is most comfortable), with an extra layer for the cool evenings. A raincoat, or at least an umbrella, will be useful in winter and spring.

Although the local people tolerate tourist habits, beach wear is not appreciated in towns and cities, and certainly not in churches. Casual dress is accepted in restaurants.

Communications

The telephone system is modern and works well. There are plenty of card-operated telephones; phonecards *(télécartes)* can be bought from post offices and *tabacs* (tobacconists). It is generally more expensive to use the phone in your hotel room, unless you use one of the calling cards issued by international telephone companies. Fax messages can be sent and received through many hotels.

The mobile phone system covers all main population centres and major roads between them, except where hampered by mountains.

To make an international call from Corsica, dial 00, then the country code (1 for the US or Canada, 44 for the UK), the area code (omitting initial zero, if any) and local number. To call anywhere in Corsica or mainland France, dial the 10-digit number.

Postal services work, although quite slowly. Airmail reaches most European destinations in 4 to 6 days. Shops that sell postcards may not have stamps; for those you will have to go to a post office, unless you can find a *tabac* which sells them.

Crime

Street crime is not likely to a problem except perhaps in the back streets of Bastia or Ajaccio, but it is always sensible to take normal precautions. Avoid dark or lonely places at night, beware of pickpockets in crowded places, don't carry large amounts of cash or wear valuable jewellery.

Theft from cars has increased, especially in cities and larger resorts in summer. Don't leave anything on show when parking your car. Use guarded car parks if you can, and leave *nothing* in a car overnight.

It is a good idea to make several photocopies of your travel tickets and passport and keep them in different places.

Driving

Drive on the right and always park pointing in the same direction as the traffic. Seat belts must

The Hard Facts

be worn, and the law requires cars to carry a red triangle to display in case of breakdown in the roadway, and a spare set of bulbs for the lights. Speed limits for cars are 50 kph (31 mph) in built-up areas, 90–100 kph (56–62 mph) outside towns and otherwise as marked.

Driving in town centres in summer can be frustrating, with frequent delays and few parking places. When visiting, find a safe parking place and walk or take taxis.

Major roads are generally good and well-surfaced; minor country and mountain roads may be poor, with hairpin bends and eroded edges. Where there's an unguarded precipice on one side and solid rock or a deep gully on the other, and no room for two cars to pass, the situation can be hair-raising! On narrow mountain roads, the locals are used to the scenery and want to go faster than the visitors. They make the point by sitting on the tail of slower cars. Don't go *too* slowly, and move in to let them pass when you can, or they may do something life-threatening.

If you have an accident, try to inform the police, or ensure that someone else does. If anyone is injured, you may be arrested until blame is allocated. If you take your own vehicle, you will need to make certain that you are fully insured—check with your insurance company or motoring organization.

Emergencies

To call the police dial 17; the fire service *(Pompiers)* 18; an ambulance 15. Do not expect the respondent to speak English.

Essentials

Be sure to take sun screen cream (a high protection factor is essential in summer), a sun hat, dark glasses, insect repellent (especially if you plan to camp), film and any medicines you may need: the same brands may not be available.

Etiquette

Always greet someone (*Bonjour, monsieur, madame* or *mademoiselle*) before saying anything else, or asking a question. It's usual to shake hands when meeting people, and when taking leave of them.

Ferries

The car ferries of SNCM Ferryterranée operate year-round between Toulon, Marseille and Nice on the French mainland and Ajaccio and Bastia. In summer, many more services are added to Propriano, Calvi, L'Ile-Rousse and Porto-Vecchio, including connections from Genoa and Livorno in Italy.

THE HARD FACTS

Bonifacio is linked to northern Sardinia by car ferry all year round.

Formalities

Citizens of European Union countries can enter with a national identity card or passport. Visas are not needed by travellers from western European countries, Japan, Canada, New Zealand or the USA.

You may take the following goods into Corsica (France) duty-free: 200 cigarettes or 50 cigars or 250 g tobacco; 1 litre of spirits (liquor) and 1 bottle of wine; a reasonable quantity of perfume and *eau de toilette*. Entering from (or returning to) other EU countries, larger quantities of tax- and duty-paid goods may be carried for personal use.

Local and foreign currency may be imported, but amounts above 50,000 francs should be declared.

Health and Medical Matters

To avoid the usual travellers' intestinal and other afflictions, start by eating moderately, and avoiding too much alcohol and too much sun. Drink plenty of water, wear a sun hat, use a sunscreen with a high protection factor (at least 20) and make sure that children do the same.

Pharmacists are always ready to give advice and will direct you to a doctor if necessary. They sell a wide variety of medications over the counter, but some will be under unfamiliar names.

It is advisable to take out comprehensive travel insurance, including coverage of medical expenses. EU nationals can get free emergency treatment; it helps if they carry a qualifying document. UK citizens should obtain the Form E111 from a post office before leaving home. Keep receipts of any payments you have to make, in order to claim refunds.

Language

French is the national language, but many people prefer to speak Corsican, which is closer to Italian. English is quite widely understood among those who often deal with visitors, but it is well worth trying to learn and put into practice a few polite phrases in French.

Media

Most hotel TVs are limited to state-run and commercial French and Italian TV channels which don't carry much of interest to foreigners. A few of the bigger hotels have satellite channels, including English and German channels.

Newspapers in English are available in the major towns; the UK papers arrive in most places on the day after publication.

The Hard Facts

Money

The currency is the *franc* (FFR or Fr), divided into 100 *centimes*, with banknotes from 20 to 500 francs and coins from 5 centimes to 20 francs. Prices may also be given in euros, which will take over officially in 2002; 1 euro = 6.55957 francs.

Foreign currency and traveller's cheques may be changed at banks, exchange offices and large hotels (at a poorer rate). Major credit cards are very widely accepted. Using them or bank cards, cash may be obtained from distributors outside banks, if you know your PIN.

Opening Hours

Museums, archaeological sites and other attractions generally open from 9 or 10 a.m. to about 7 p.m. in summer. Some close on Monday or Tuesday and public holidays, and many close from noon to 2 p.m. In winter they close earlier, at 4 or 5 p.m., and some may not open at all. It is worth trying to find out in advance.

Shops open Tuesday to Saturday from 9 or 9.30 a.m. to noon, and again from 2 to 7 p.m. In summer, in tourist areas, they may open on Sunday and Monday too. Post offices open Monday to Friday from 9 a.m. to noon, 2 to 5 p.m., Saturday 9 a.m. to noon.

Banks open Monday to Friday from 8.30 a.m. to noon, and 2 to 4.30 p.m. Exchange offices keep longer hours.

Photography and Video

Colour print film is widely available and can be processed locally. Transparency film is harder to find, and it is best taken back to your own country for processing.

Video tape is available. Pre-recorded tapes are compatible with most of Europe, but not the USA.

Public Holidays

When a national holiday falls on a Tuesday or Thursday, the intervening Monday or Friday is usually taken off to make a long weekend. This practice is called *faire le pont,* roughly meaning "bridging the gap".

1 January	*Jour de l'An*
1 May	*Fête du Travail*
8 May	*Armistice 1945*
14 July	*Fête nationale*
15 August	*Assomption*
1 November	*Toussaint*
11 November	*Armistice 1918*
25 December	*Noël*

Moveable:

March–April	*lundi de Pâques* (Easter Monday)
April–May	*Ascension*
May–June	*lundi de Pentecôte* (Whit Monday)

Public Transport

Regular bus services run between all the main towns, starting from central bus stations or the company's own terminal. Within cities, taxis are readily available. If they don't have meters, agree on the fare in advance.

A narrow-gauge railway train runs across the island from Ajaccio via Corte to Bastia. A branch line links Calvi with Ponte Leccia, north of Corte. Tourist offices have pocket timetables. Note that at many stations the trains stop only on request. You need to wave one down if you wish to board, and press the signal to the driver if you are on the train and want to get off.

Religion

The majority of people are Catholic, although church attendance is in decline amongst the younger generation and some teaching—such as that on birth control—is widely ignored. In addition there are various Protestant churches and synagogues in the main cities.

Time

GMT +1 in winter, +2 in summer, one hour ahead of the UK and Ireland.

Tipping

Restaurant bills include a service charge; a tip is not expected. In informal bars and cafés, it's the custom to leave some small change. Taxi drivers expect fares to be rounded up by about 10%, and a small tip is usually given to porters. Cloakroom attendants generally leave a saucer in an obvious place for a few coins.

Toilets

Variously labelled *toilettes* or WC, clean public lavatories are provided at most tourist attractions. Bars and cafés may have them—it is polite to buy a drink or coffee or leave a coin or two if you use one of those.

Tourist Information

Airports and major towns have tourist offices, typically open Monday to Saturday from 9 or 10 a.m. to noon and 2 to 7 p.m. Most of them have good information leaflets and maps.

Voltage

The electrical supply is 220 volts AC, 50 Hz. Plugs are of the mainland European type, with two round pins. Any 110-volt equipment needs a transformer as well as an adaptor.

Water

Tap water is safe to drink unless marked otherwise (*Non potable* means "not drinkable"), although many people prefer bottled mineral water.

INDEX

Agriates, désert 43
Aitone, forêt 21
Ajaccio 11–15
Aléria 31–32
Algajola 45–46
Aregno 45–46
Asco, vallée 35
Bastelica 16
Bastia 37–38
Bavella, col 31
Bonifacio 27–29
Calacuccia 22
Calanche 19
Calenzana 47
Calvi 46–47
Cap Corse 39–42
Cargèse 18
Castagniccia 35
Centuri-Port 41
Cervione 35
Cinarca 17
Corte 33–34
Erbalunga 41
Ficajola 18
Filitosa 9, 23–24
Galéria 47
Girolata 20
Iles Lavezzi 29
–Sanguinaires 15
La Canonica 39
La Marana 39
Lavasina 39–41
Lavezzi, îles 29
L'Ile-Rousse 45
L'Ospédale 30
Macinaggio 41
Mariana 39
Marine-de-Sisco 41
Megalithic sites 23–25
Morosaglia 35
Murato 42–43
Nebbio 42–43
Niolo 22
Nonza 41–42
Oletta 42
Partinello 20–21
Piana 18
Porticcio 15
Porto 19–20
Porto-Vecchio 30
Propriano 23
Prunelli, gorges 15–16
Restonica, vallée 34
Rondinara, plage 29
Route des Artisans 46
Sagone 17–18
Saint-Florent 42
Sampiero Corso 16
Sant'Antonino 46
Sartène 24–25
Scala di Santa Regina 22
Scandola Peninsula 28
Solenzara 31
Spelunca, gorges 21
Tavignano, gorges 34
Tiuccia 17
Vergio, col 21–22
Zonza 31

General editor: Barbara Ender-Jones
Editor: Alice Taucher
Layout: Luc Malherbe
Photos: covers, pp. 14, 19, 26, 45, 52 Hémisphères/Wysocki;
pp. 6, 10, 24, 32, 36, 40, 56 Bernard Joliat
Maps: Elsner & Schichor, Huber Kartographie

Copyright © 1999 by JPM Publications S.A.
12, avenue William-Fraisse, 1006 Lausanne, Switzerland
E-mail: information@jpmguides.com
Web site: http://www.jpmguides.com/

All rights reserved. No part of this book may be reproduced or transmitted in any form or by any means, electronic or mechanical, including photocopying, recording or by any information storage and retrieval system without permission in writing from the publisher.

Every care has been taken to verify the information in the guide, but the publisher cannot accept responsibility for any errors that may have occurred. If you spot an inaccuracy or a serious omission, please let us know. Printed in Switzerland—Gessler